CONTENTS

Abide with Me

Electronic Organs

Upper: Fr. Horn (Fl.) 8'
Lower: Strings 8', 4'
Pedal: Soft 16' to Gt.

Tonebar Organ

Upper: 00 0840 000 (00)
Lower: (00) 5533 200 (0)
Pedal: 4 (0) 2 (0) (Spinet 3)

Words by Henry F. Lyte
Music by William H. Monk

* A slight pause between these phrases increases the effectiveness.

FIRST 50 SONGS

YOU SHOULD PLAY ON THE ORGAN

ISBN 978-1-5400-4466-2

Visit Hal Leonard Online at
www.halleonard.com

Contact us:
Hal Leonard
7777 West Bluemound Road
Milwaukee, WI 53213
Email: info@halleonard.com

In Europe, contact:
Hal Leonard Europe Limited
42 Wigmore Street
Marylebone, London, W1U 2RN
Email: info@halleonardeurope.com

In Australia, contact:
Hal Leonard Australia Pty. Ltd.
4 Lentara Court
Cheltenham, Victoria, 3192 Australia
Email: info@halleonard.com.au

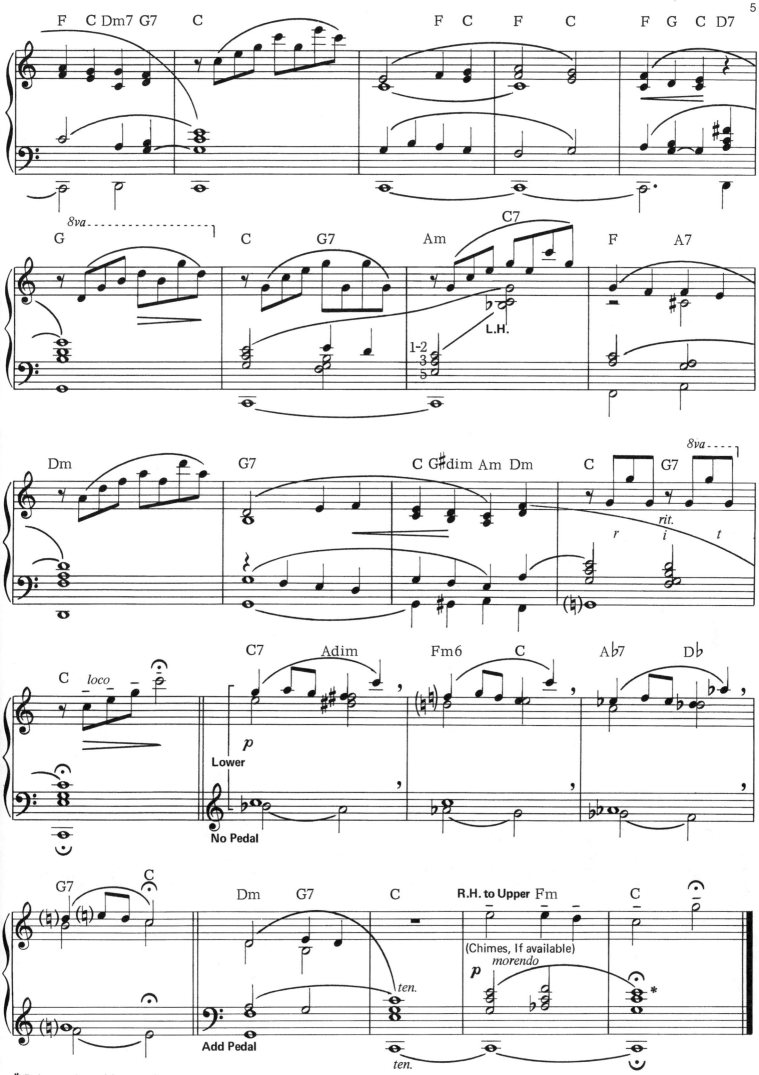

* Release when chime expires.

All I Ask Of You
from PHANTOM OF THE OPERA

Electronic Organs

Upper: Flutes (or Tibias) 16', 8', 4'
Lower: Melodia 8', Reed 8'
Pedal: 8'
Vib./Trem.: On, Fast

Drawbar Organs

Upper: 80 4800 00
Lower: (00) 7334 011
Pedal: 15
Vib./Trem.: On, Fast

Music by Andrew Lloyd Webber
Lyrics by Charles Hart
Additional Lyrics by Richard Stilgoe

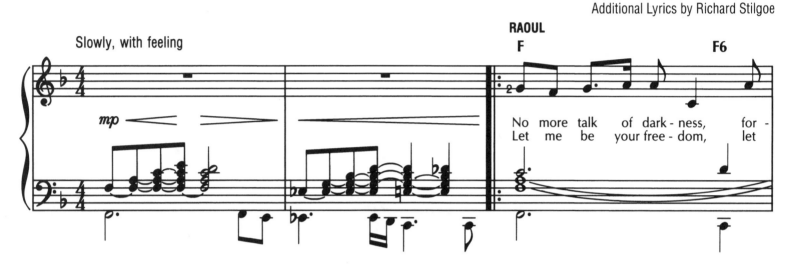

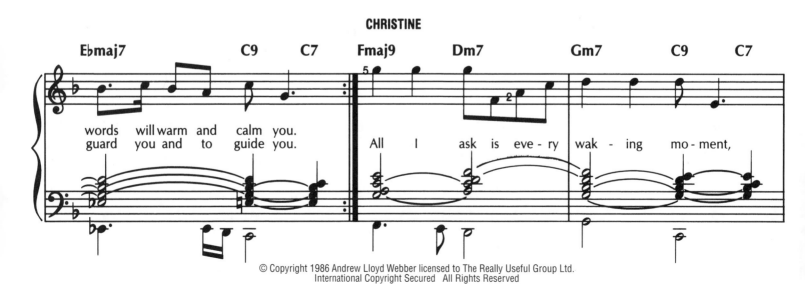

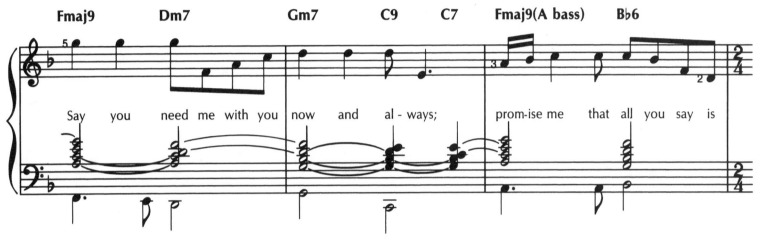

CHRISTINE

E♭maj7   C9   C7   F6   Fmaj7   F6

fears are far be-hind you. All I want is free-dom, a world with no more night; and

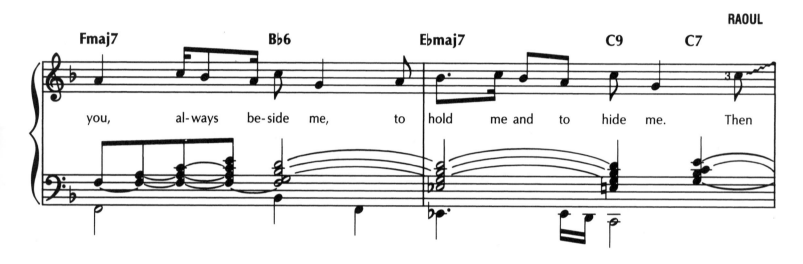

RAOUL

Fmaj7   B♭6   E♭maj7   C9   C7

you, al-ways be-side me, to hold me and to hide me. Then

Fmaj9   Dm7   Gm7   C9 C7   F(A bass)   Dm7

say you'll share with me one love, one life-time; let me lead you from your

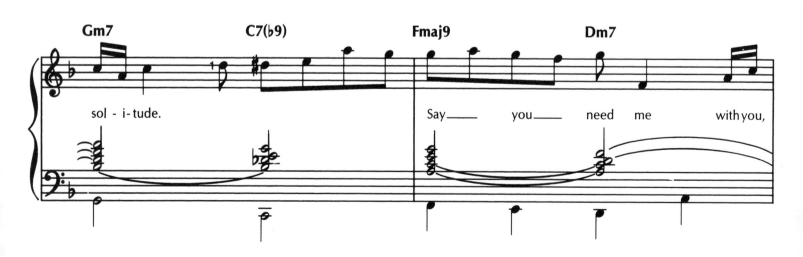

Gm7   C7(♭9)   Fmaj9   Dm7

sol-i-tude. Say___ you___ need me with you,

All My Loving

Electronic Organs
Upper: Flutes (or Tibias) 16′, 8′, 5⅓′,
      4′, 2′
Lower: Flutes 8′, 4′, Diapason 8′
      Reed 8′
Pedal: String Bass
Vib./Trem.: On, Fast

Tonebar Organs
Upper: 86 6606 000
Lower: (00) 7732 211
Pedal: String Bass
Vib./Trem.: On Fast

Words and Music by John Lennon
and Paul McCartney

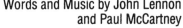

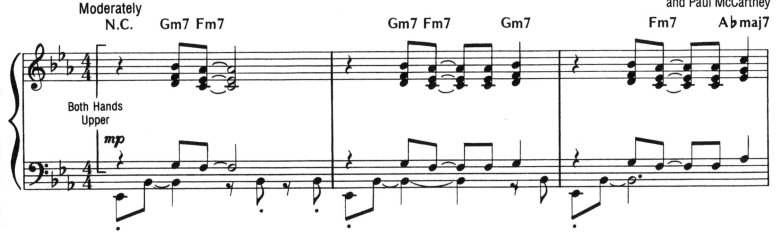

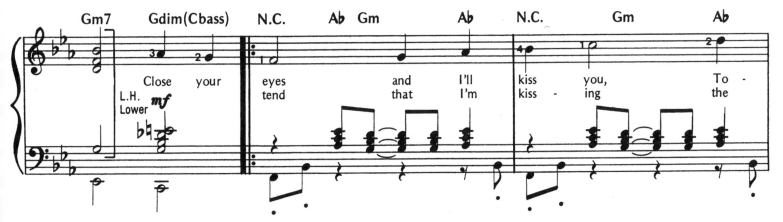

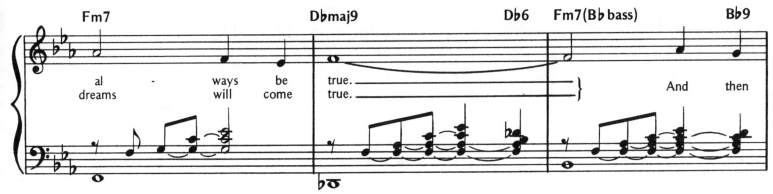

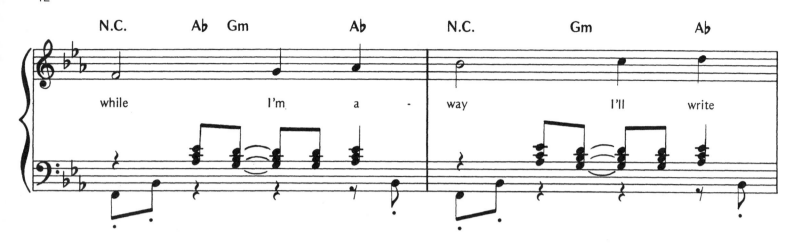

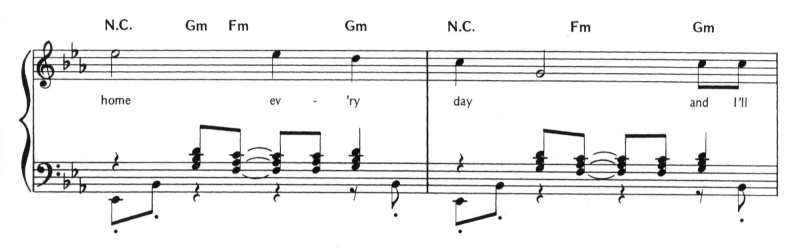

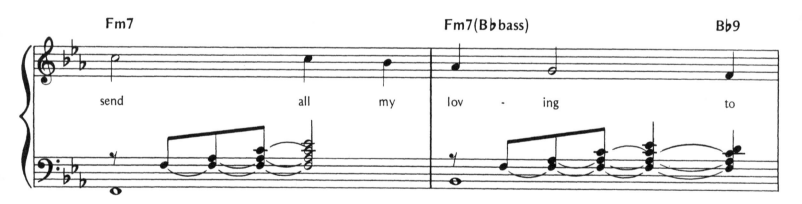

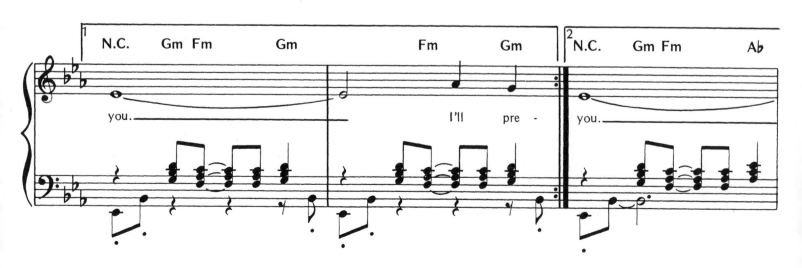

Always

Electronic Organs
Upper: Flutes (or Tibias) 16', 8'
      String 4'
Lower: Flute 8', Diapason 8', String 8'
Pedal: 16', 8'
Vib./Trem.: On, Slow

Drawbar Organs
Upper: 81 5505 004
Lower: (00) 7343 312
Pedal: 26
Vib./Trem.: On, Slow

Words and Music by
Irving Berlin

Moderate Waltz

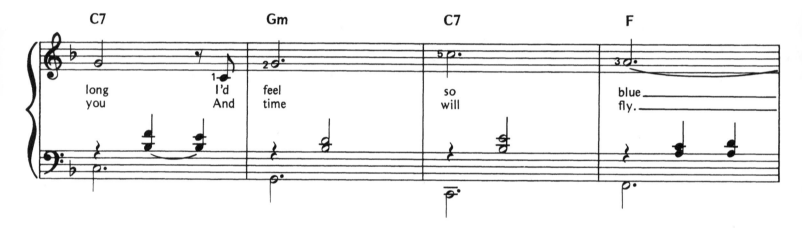

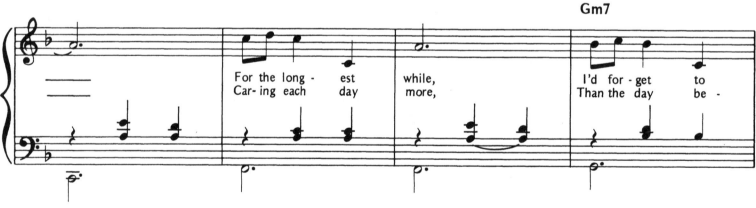

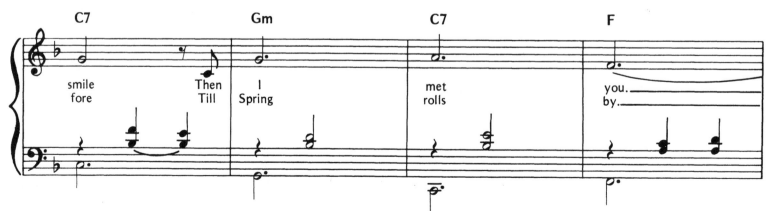

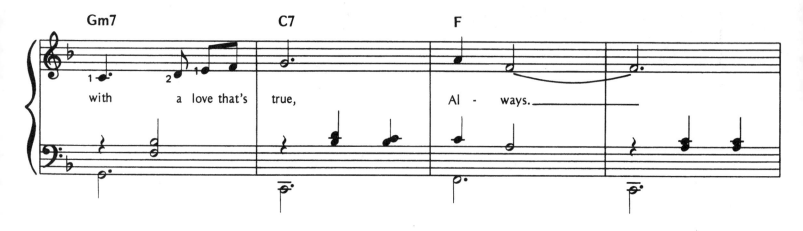

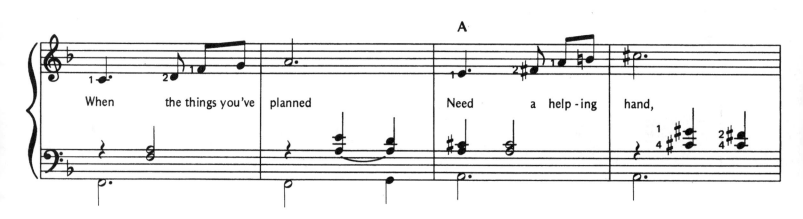

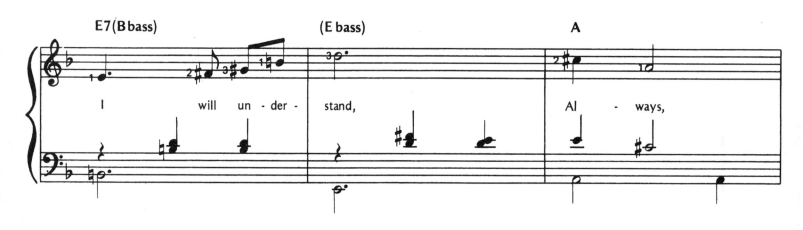

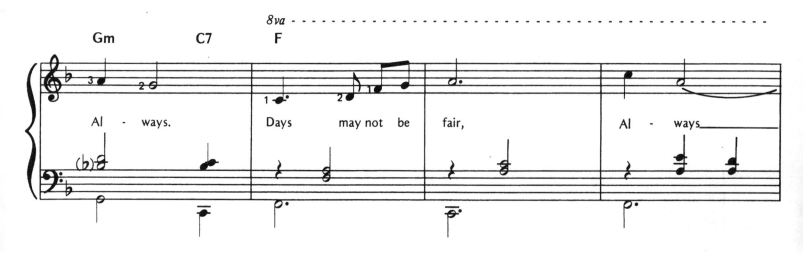

America, the Beautiful

Electronic and Pipe Organs

Upper: Full, with 16' and Light Reed(s)
Lower: Op. Diap. 8', Vln. Diap. 8', Fl. 8'
       (8' Stgs. if needed)
Pedal: 16' and 8' to balance

Drawbar Organs

Upper: 45 7654 432 (00)
Lower: (00) 8876 543 (0)
Pedal: 7 (0) 5 (0) (Spinet 6)

Words by Katherine Lee Bates
Music by Samuel A. Ward

*Play detached (**not** staccato) except where slurred.

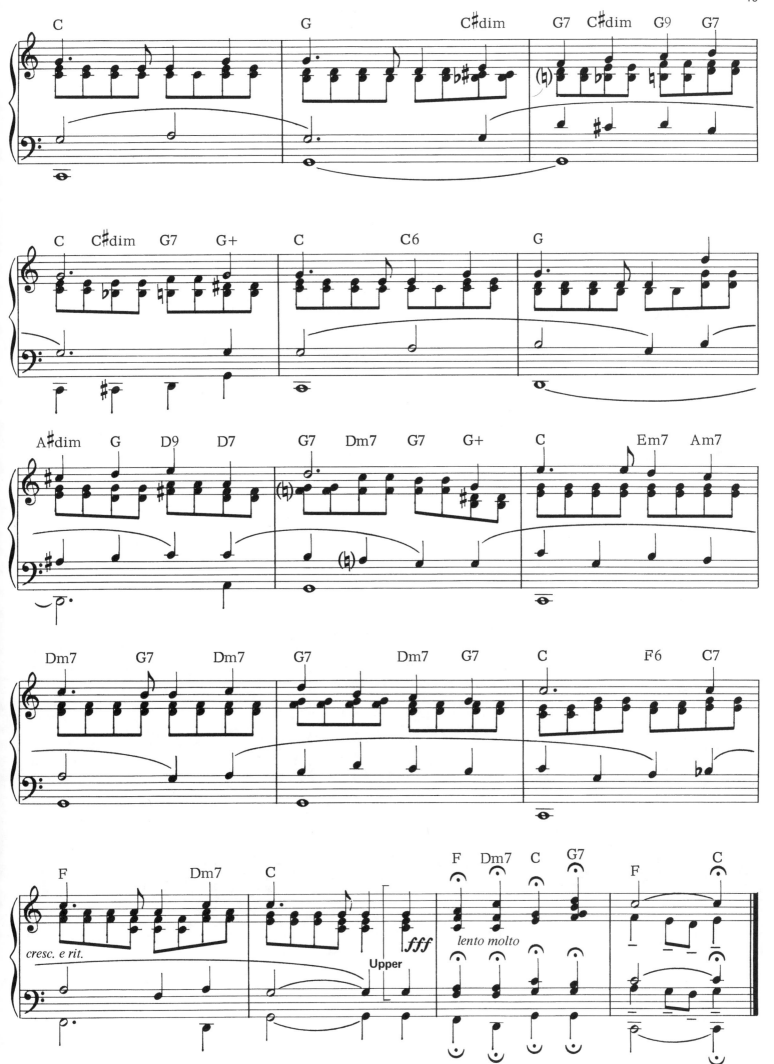

Battle Hymn of the Republic

Electronic and Pipe Organs

Upper: *ff*, no heavy reeds
Lower: *ff*, with solo reeds
Pedal: *ff* to Sw.

Drawbar Organs

Upper: 40 6678 452 (00)
Lower: (00) 8876 543 (0)
Pedal: 7 (0) 5 (0) (Spinet 6)

Words by Julia Ward Howe
Music by William Steffe

Andante maestoso - with well-defined rhythm

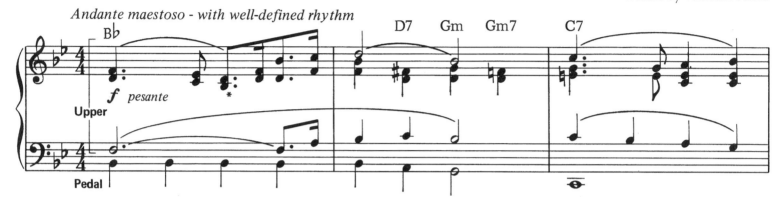

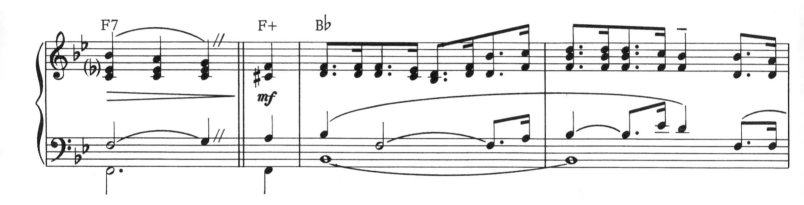

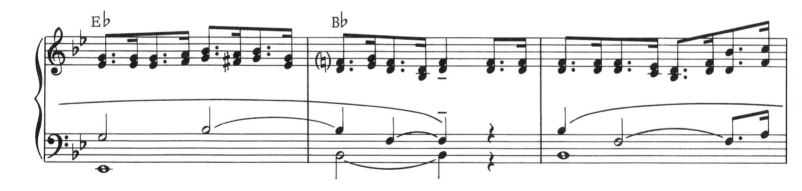

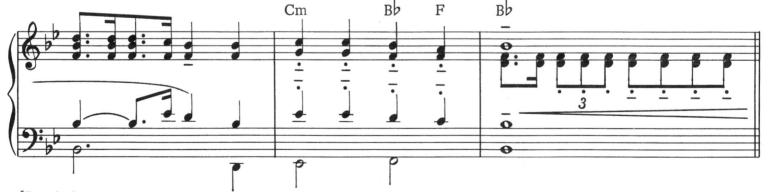

*Detached, **not** staccato

Beauty and the Beast
from BEAUTY AND THE BEAST

Electronic Organs

Upper: Flute 4'
Lower: Strings
Pedal: Bass 8' or
    Elec. bass (soft)
Vib./Trem.: On, Fast

Drawbar Organs

Upper: 60 0608 008
Lower: (00) 6500 001
Pedal: 05
Vib./Trem.: On, fast

Lyrics by HOWARD ASHMAN
Music by ALAN MENKEN

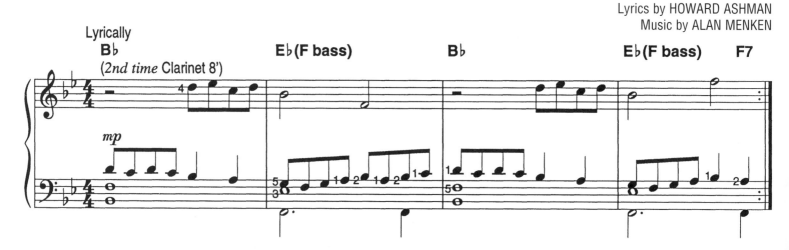

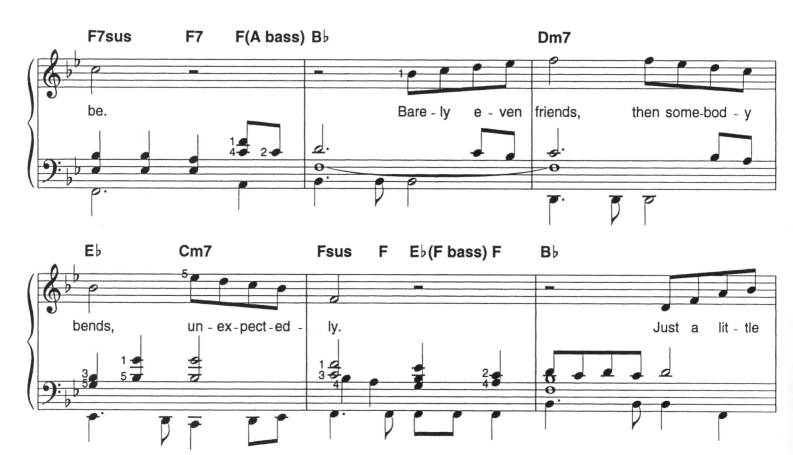

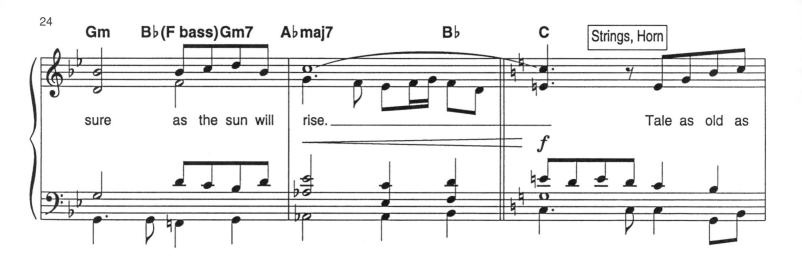

sure as the sun will rise. _____ Tale as old as

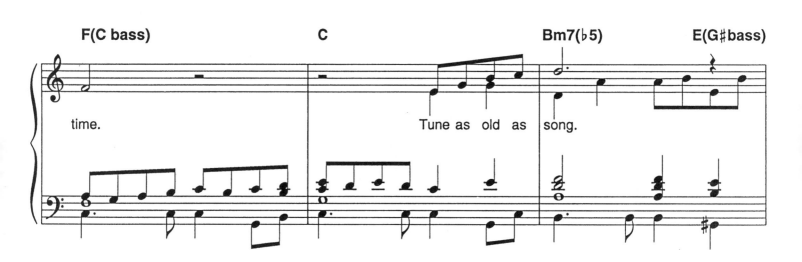

time. Tune as old as song.

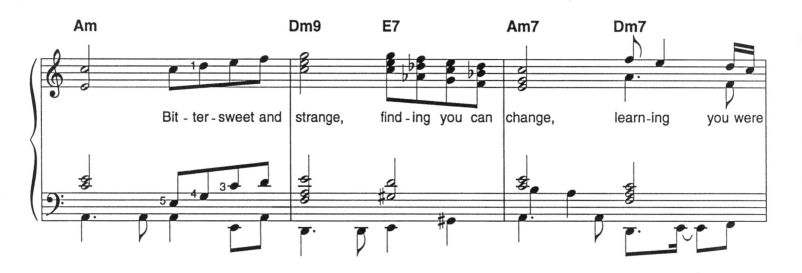

Bit-ter-sweet and strange, find-ing you can change, learn-ing you were

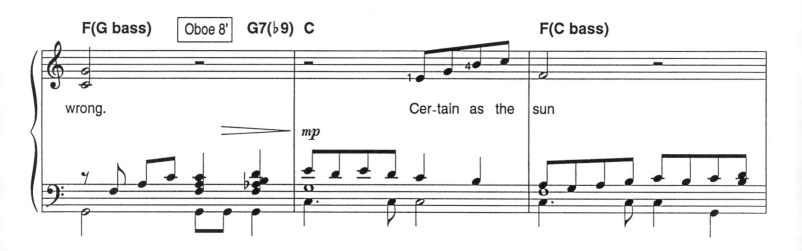

wrong. Cer-tain as the sun

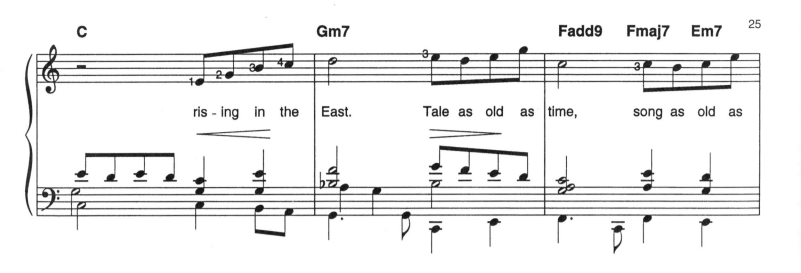

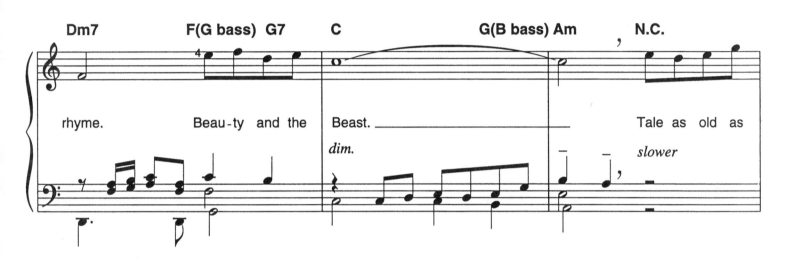

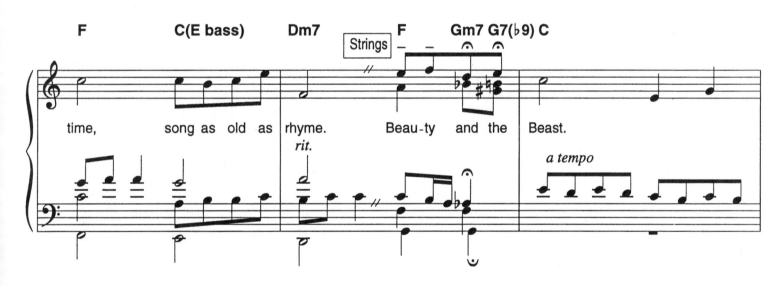

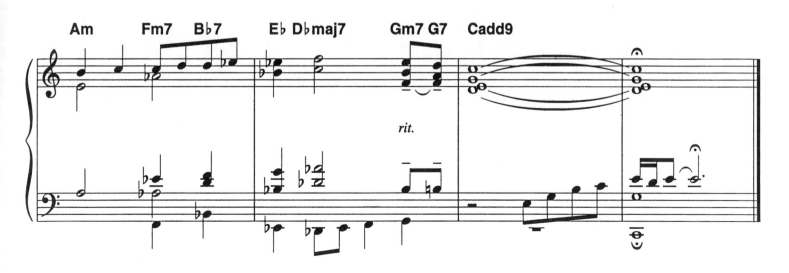

Bring Him Home
from LES MISÉRABLES

Electronic Organs
Upper: Flutes (or Tibias) 16', 4'
Lower: Strings 8', 4'
Pedal: 16', 8'
Vib./Trem.: On, Fast

Drawbar Organs
Upper: 60 3616 003
Lower: (00) 5677 654
Pedal: 33
Vib./Trem.: On, Fast

Music by Claude-Michel Schönberg
Lyrics by Herbert Kretzmer and Alain Boublil

Slowly, with feeling

Circle of Life
from THE LION KING

Electronic Organs
Upper: Flutes (or Tibias) 8', 4'
      Horn 8'
Lower: Melodia 8', Reed 8'
Pedal: String Bass
Vib./Trem.: On, Fast

Drawbar Organs
Upper: 53 6606 000
Lower: (00) 7400 011
Pedal: String Bass
Vib./Trem.: On, Fast

Music by ELTON JOHN
Lyrics by TIM RICE

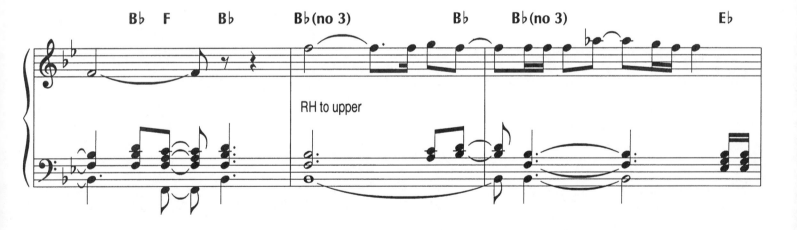

Same tempo, gently and rhythmically

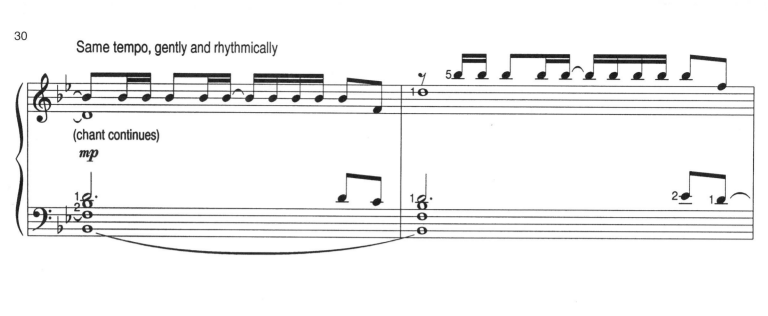

(chant continues)

mp

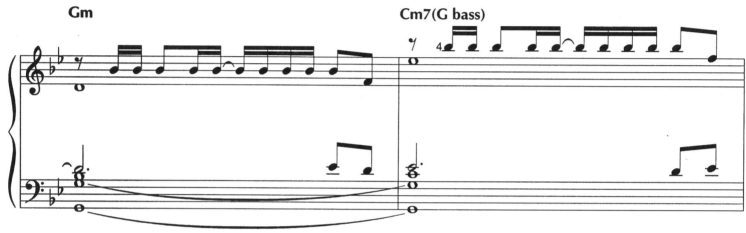

Gm   Cm7(G bass)

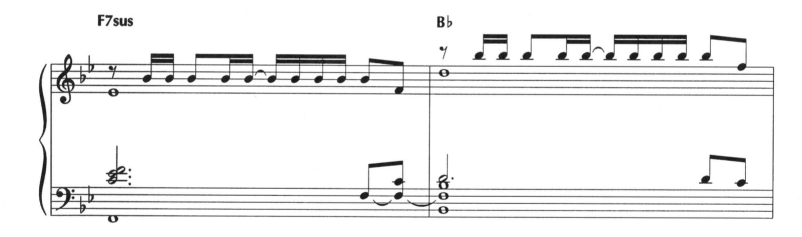

F7sus   B♭

Gm   Cm7(G bass)

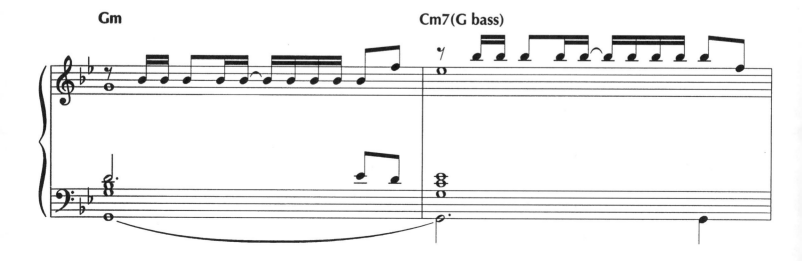

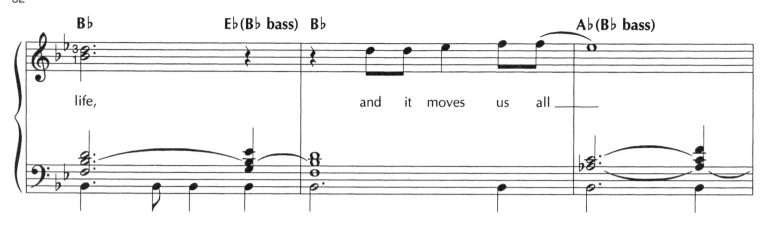

life, and it moves us all

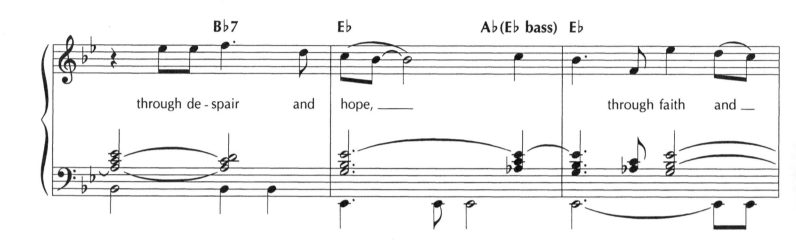

through de-spair and hope, _____ through faith and _____

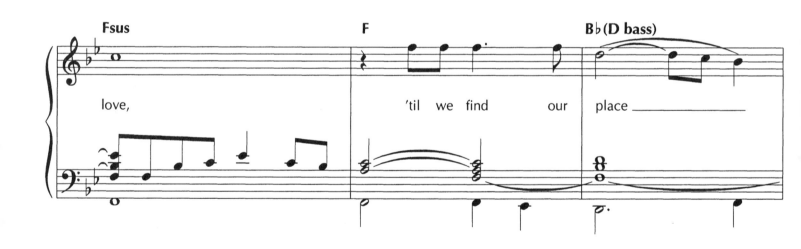

love, 'til we find our place _____

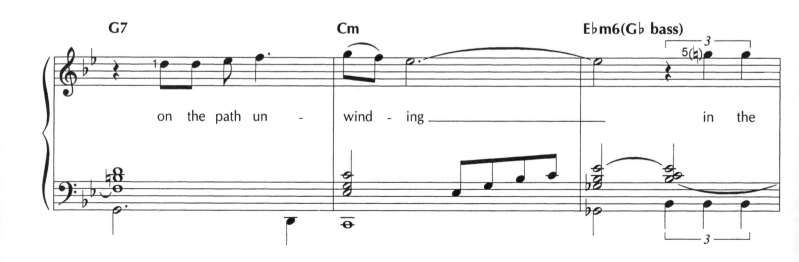

on the path un-wind - ing _____ in the

ADD VIOLIN

It's the cir - cle of life,

and it moves us all _____ through de - spair and _____

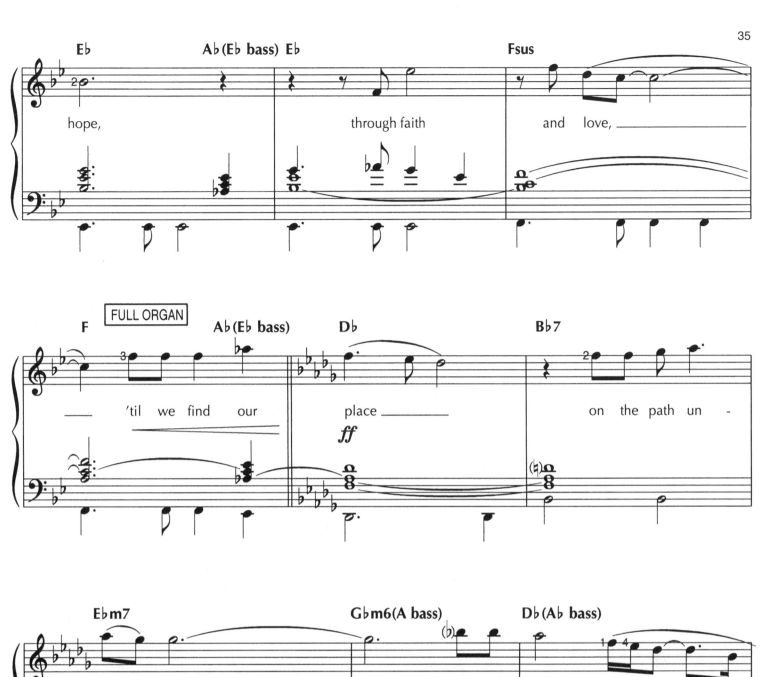

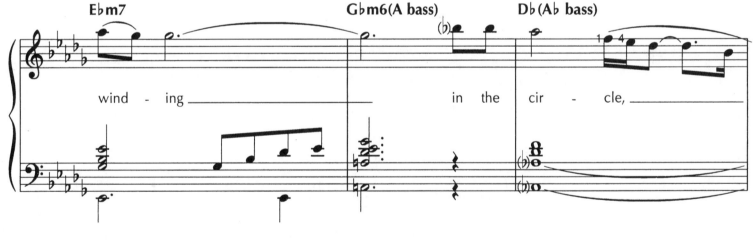

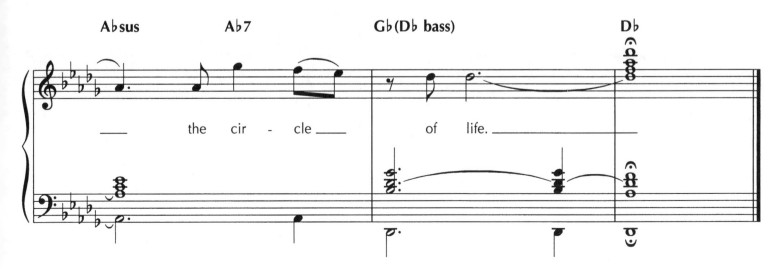

Can You Feel the Love Tonight

from THE LION KING

Electronic Organs
Upper: Flute (or Tibia) 4'
      Clarinet 8'
Lower: Strings 8', 4'
Pedal: 16', 8'
Vib./Trem.: On, Fast

Drawbar Organs
Upper: 53 5864 101
Lower: (00) 7104 000
Pedal: 35
Vib./Trem.: On, Fast

Music by ELTON JOHN
Lyrics by TIM RICE

CODA

City of Stars
from LA LA LAND

Electronic Organs
Upper: Flutes (or Tibias) 16', 8', 4', 2'
        Strings 8', 4'
Lower: Flutes 8', 4'
        String 8', 4'
Pedal: 16', 8'
Vib./Trem.: On, Fast

Drawbar Organs
Upper: 82 5325 004
Lower: (00) 7345 312
Pedal: 44
Vib./Trem.: On, Fast

Music by Justin Hurwitz
Lyrics by Benj Pasek & Justin Paul

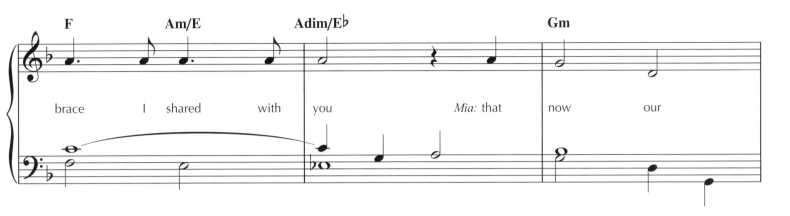

brace   I   shared   with   you   *Mia:* that   now   our

dreams   may   fi - n'lly   come   true. _____

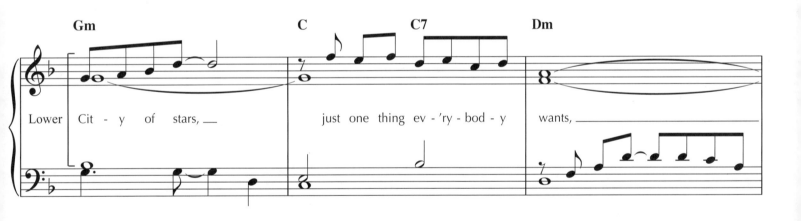

Lower | Cit - y   of   stars, ___   just   one   thing   ev - 'ry - bod - y   wants, _____

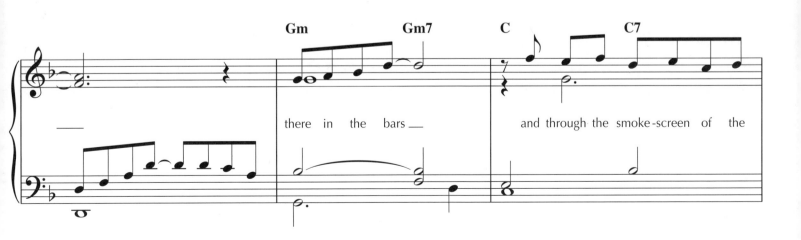

___   there   in   the   bars ___   and   through   the   smoke-screen   of   the

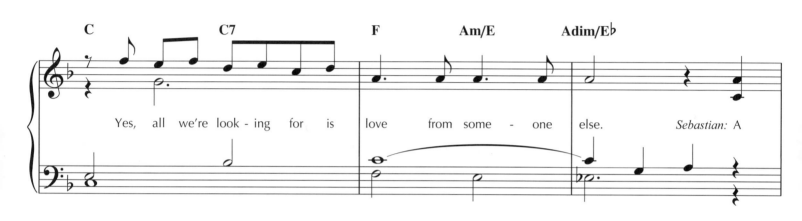

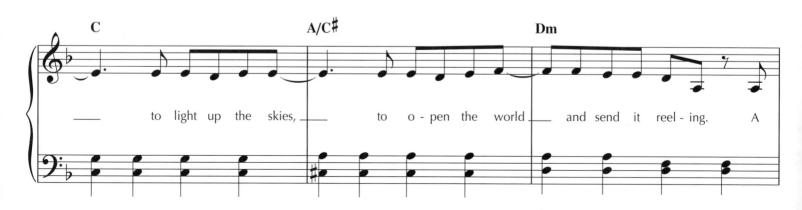

voice that says, "I'll be here, ___ and you'll be al - right." ___

I don't care if I know ___ just where I will go, ___

___ 'cause all that I need's ___ this cra - zy feel - ing, a rat - tat - tat on my heart... ___

Sebastian: Think I want it to stay. ___

ped.

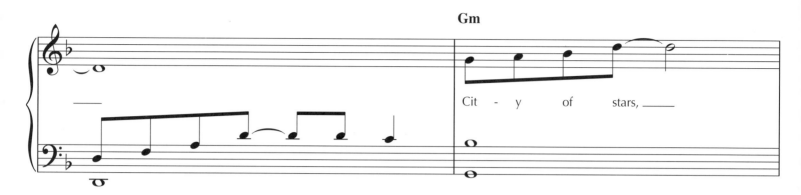

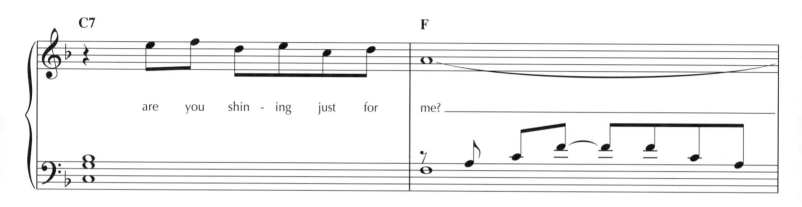

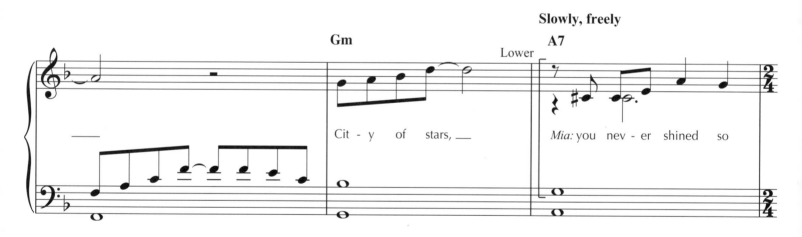

Evermore
from BEAUTY AND THE BEAST

Electronic Organs
Upper: Flutes (or Tibias) 16', 8', 4'
Lower: Melodia 8', Reed 8'
Pedal: 8'
Vib./Trem.: On, Fast

Drawbar Organs
Upper: 80 4800 00
Lower: (00) 7334 011
Pedal: 15
Vib./Trem.: On, Fast

Music by Alan Menken
Lyrics by Tim Rice

Moderately slow, with freedom

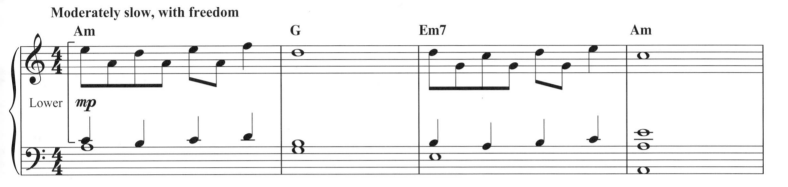

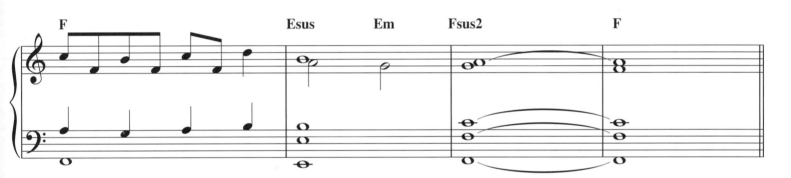

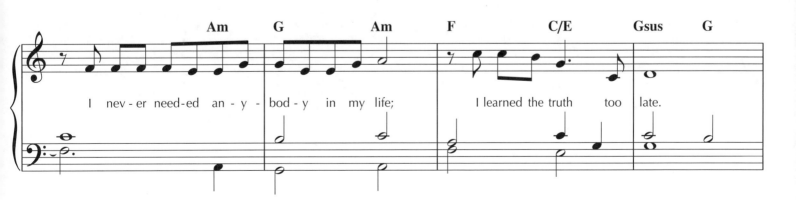

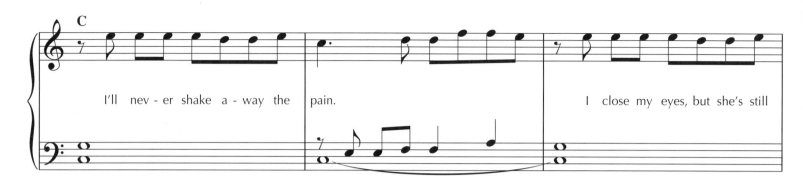

I'll nev-er shake a-way the pain. I close my eyes, but she's still

there. I let her steal in-to my mel-an-chol-y heart; it's more than I can

bear. _____ Lower Now I know she'll nev-er leave me, e-ven

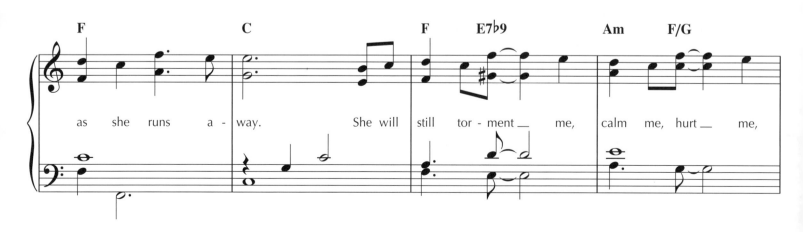

as she runs a-way. She will still tor-ment ___ me, calm me, hurt ___ me,

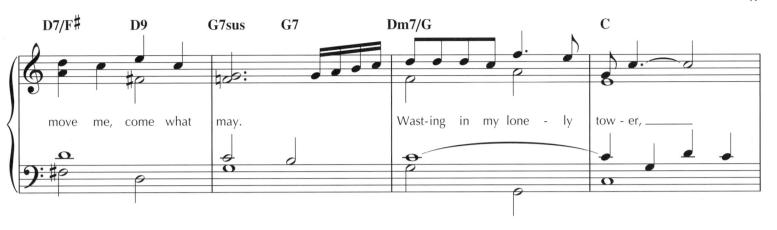

move me, come what may. Wast-ing in my lone - ly tow - er, _____

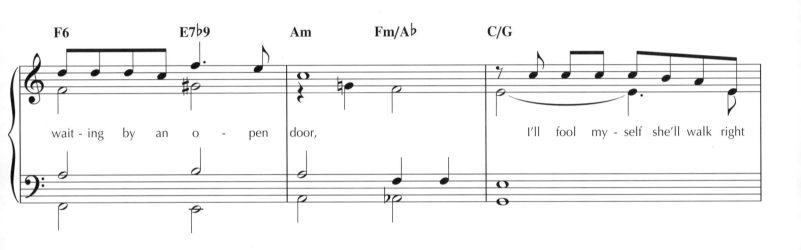

wait - ing by an o - pen door, I'll fool my - self she'll walk right

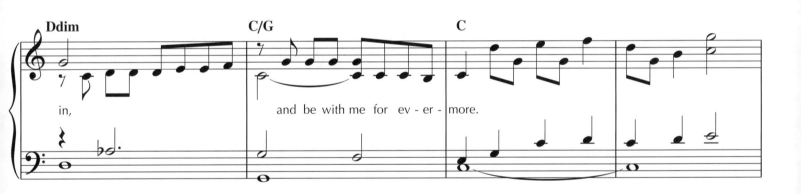

in, and be with me for ev - er - more.

I rage against the trials of love. I curse the fad-ing of the light.

Though she's al-read-y flown so far be-yond my reach, she's nev-er out of

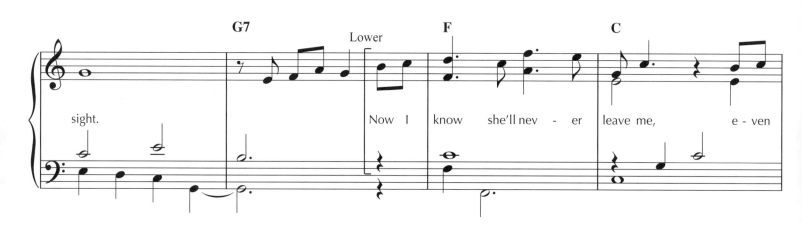

sight. Now I know she'll nev-er leave me, e-ven

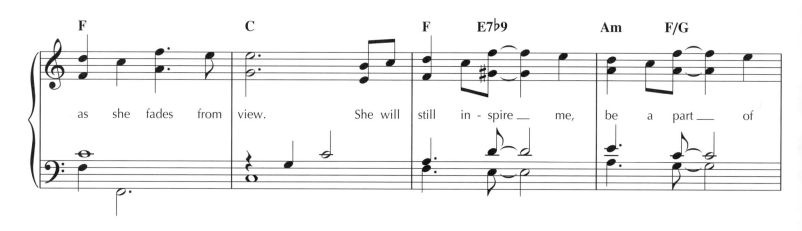

as she fades from view. She will still in-spire __ me, be a part __ of

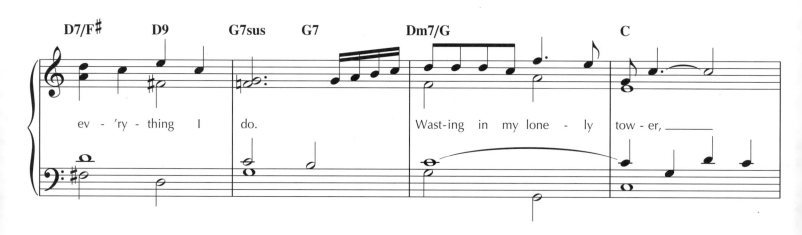

ev-'ry-thing I do. Wast-ing in my lone-ly tow-er, __

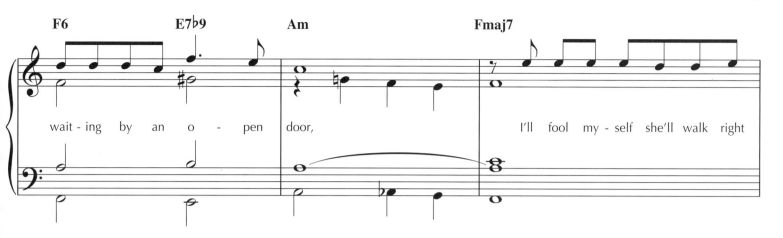

waiting by an o - pen door,   I'll fool my-self she'll walk right

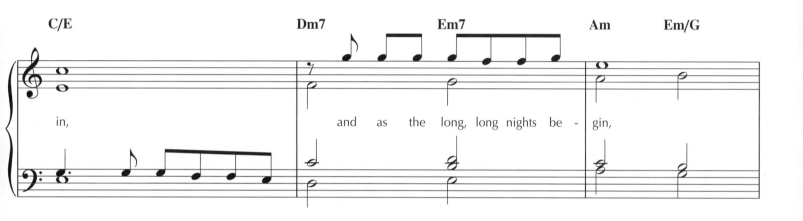

in,   and as the long, long nights be - gin,

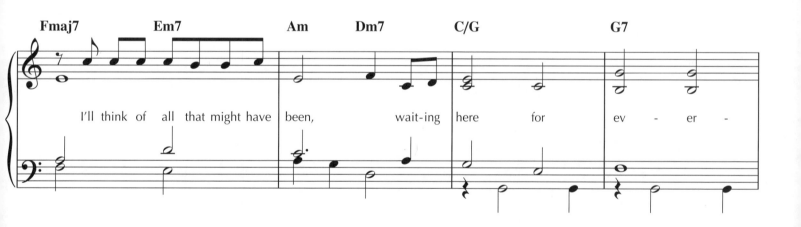

I'll think of all that might have been,   wait-ing here for   ev - er -

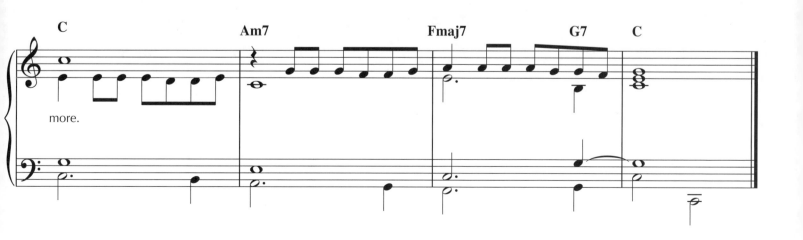

more.

Climb Ev'ry Mountain
from THE SOUND OF MUSIC

Electronic Organs
Upper: Flute (or Tibia) 8′
Lower: Diapason 8′
Pedal: 8′
Vib./Trem.: On, Fast

Drawbar Organs
Upper: 00 8300 000
Lower: (00) 6502 000
Pedal: 04
Vib./Trem.: On, Fast

Lyrics by Oscar Hammerstein II
Music by Richard Rodgers

With deep feeling

Climb ev-'ry moun-tain, search high and low,
Fol-low ev-'ry by-way, ev-'ry path you know.
Climb ev-'ry moun-tain, ford ev-'ry stream,
Fol-low ev-'ry rain-bow, till you find your

Do You Hear The People Sing?
from LES MISÉRABLES

Electronic Organs
Upper: Trumpet
Lower: Strings 8', 4'
Pedal: 16', 8'
Vib./Trem.: On, Fast

Drawbar Organs
Upper: 86 8765 021
Lower: (00) 5677 654
Pedal: 45
Vib./Trem.: On, Fast

Music by Claude-Michel Schönberg
Lyrics by Alain Boublil, Jean-Marc Natel
and Herbert Kretzmer

Edelweiss
from THE SOUND OF MUSIC

Electronic Organs
Upper: Flute (or Tibia) 4'
      Sustain
Lower: Flute 8'
Pedal: 8'
Vib./Trem.: On, Fast

Drawbar Organs
Upper: 00 0600 000
Lower: (00) 7000 000
Pedal: 05
Vib./Trem.: On, Fast

Lyrics by Oscar Hammerstein II
Music by Richard Rodgers

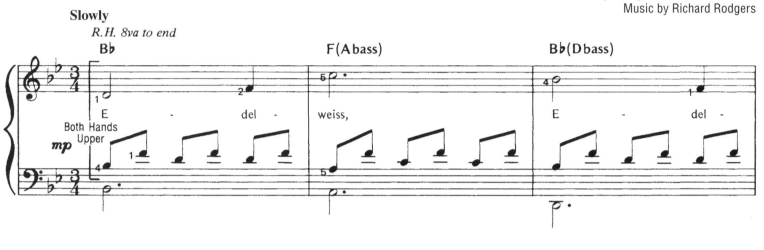

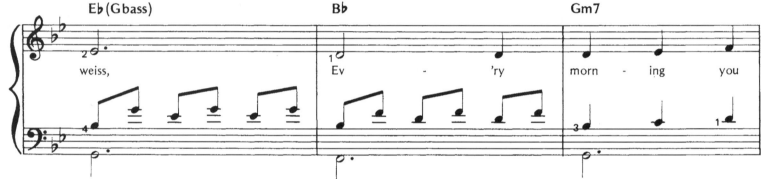

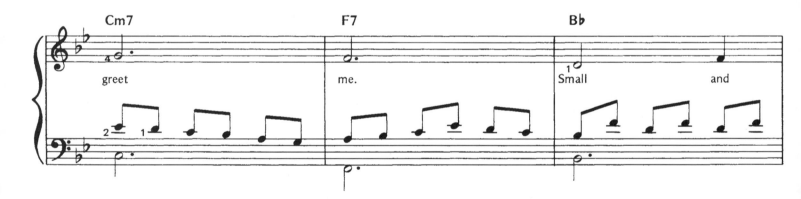

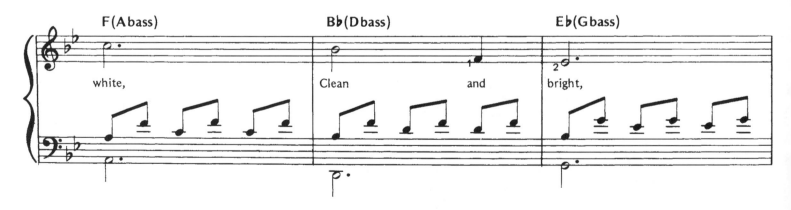

Eleanor Rigby

Electronic Organs
Upper: Flutes (or Tibias) 16', 8', 4', 2
       String 8', 4'
Lower: Flutes 8', 4'
       String 8', 4'
Pedal: 16', 8'
Vib./Trem.: On, Fast

Tonebar Organs
Upper: 82 5325 004
Lower: (00) 7345 312
Pedal: 44
Vib./Trem.: On, Fast

Words and Music by John Lennon
and Paul McCartney

Moderately

Ah_____ look at all____ the lone-ly peo - ple!_____

1,3 E - lea - nor Rig - by,____ picks up the rice____ in the church
2 Fath-er Mc Ken - zie,____ writ-ing the words____ of a ser -

No Pedal

____ where a wed-ing has been, lives in a dream.____
- mon that no - one will hear, no one comes near.____

Pedal

Waits at the win - dow,____ wear-ing the face____ that she keeps
Look at him work - ing,____ darn-ing his socks____ in the night

No pedal

Endless Love

Electronic Organs
Upper: Flutes (or Tibias) 16', 8', 4', 2',
        String 8', 4'
Lower: Flutes 8', 4',
        Strings 8', 4'
Pedal: 16', 8'
Vib./Trem.: On, Fast

Drawbar Organs
Upper: 82 5325 004
Lower: (00) 7345 312
Pedal: 44
Vib./Trem.: On, Fast

Words and Music by
Lionel Richie

Slowly - with an easy flow

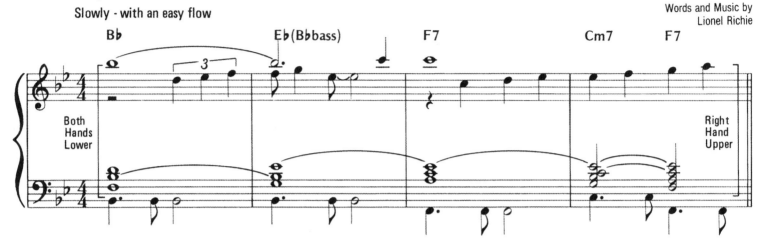

8va second time

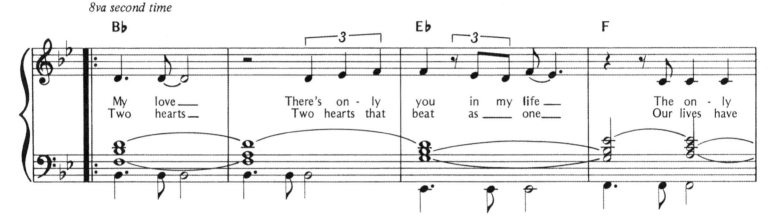

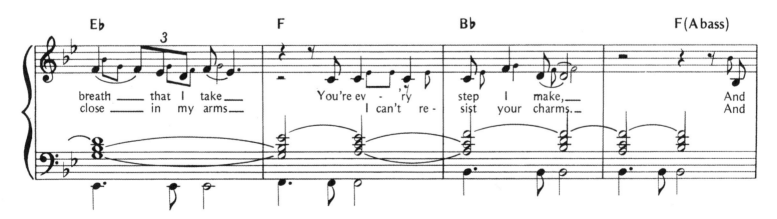

Fly Me to the Moon
(In Other Words)

Electronic Organs
Upper: Flutes (or Tibias) 16', 2'
        Add Percussion
Lower: Flutes 8', 4'
Pedal: 16'
Vib./Trem.: On, Slow

Drawbar Organs
Upper: 80 0400 304
Lower: (00) 7404 203
Pedal: 53
Vib./Trem.: On, Slow

Words and Music by
Bart Howard

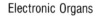

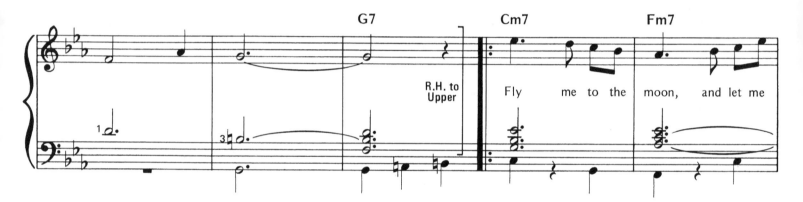

The Good, the Bad and the Ugly
(Main Title)
from THE GOOD, THE BAD AND THE UGLY

Electronic Organs
Upper: Flute (or Tibia) 4'
        Sustain
Lower: Flute 8'
Pedal: 8'
Vib./Trem.: On, Fast

Drawbar Organs
Upper: 00 0600 000
Lower: (00) 7000 000
Pedal: 05
Vib./Trem.: On, Fast

By Ennio Morricone

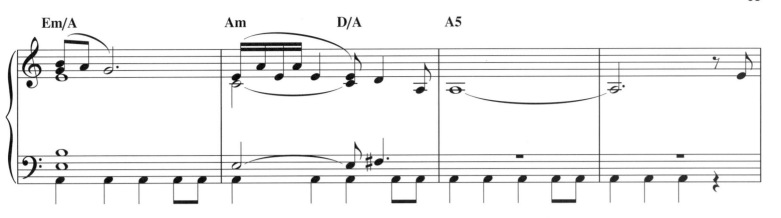

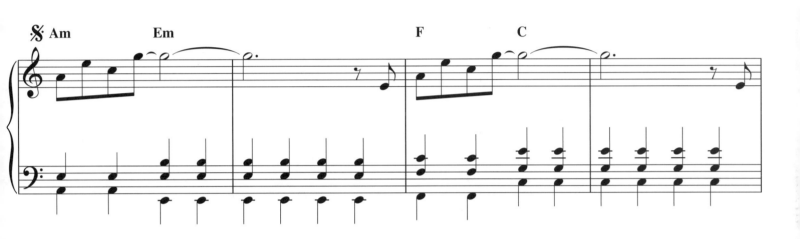

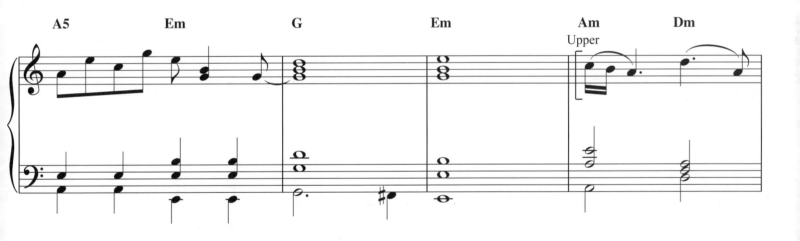

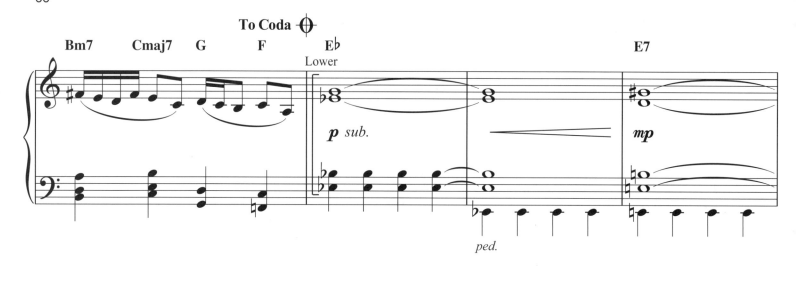

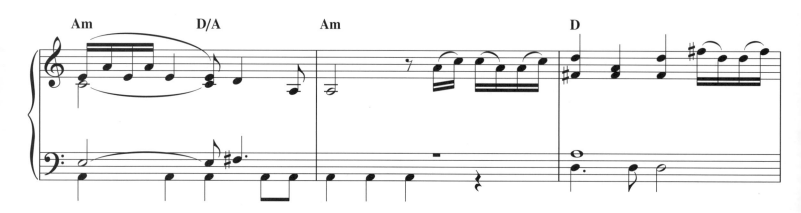

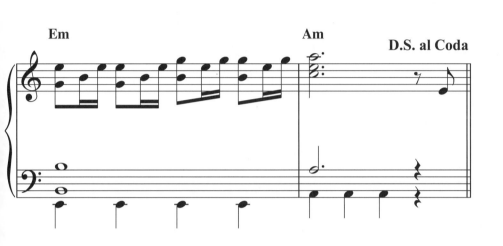

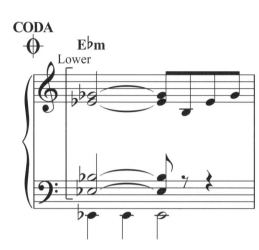

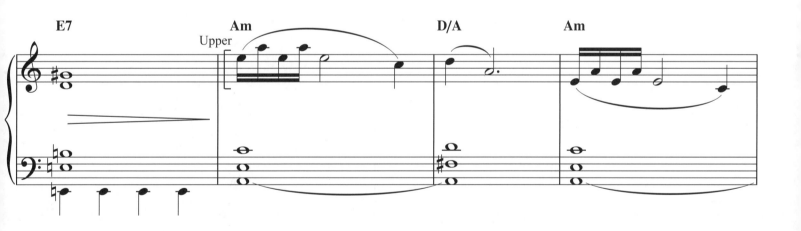

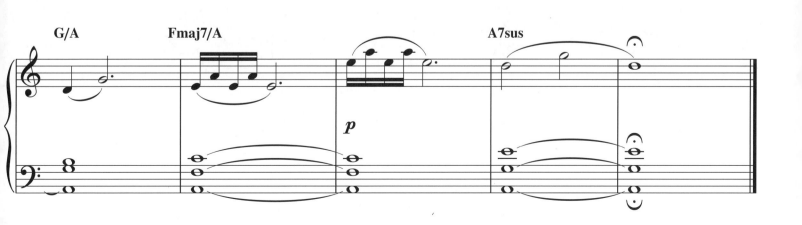

Green Onions

Electronic Organs
Upper: Clarinet 8'
Lower: Flutes 8', 4'
Pedal: 16', 8'
Vib./Trem.: On, Fast

Drawbar Organs
Upper: 80 8800 001
Lower: (00) 8404 003
Pedal: 34
Vib./Trem.: On, Fast

Written by Al Jackson, Jr.,
Lewis Steinberg, Booker T. Jones
and Steve Cropper

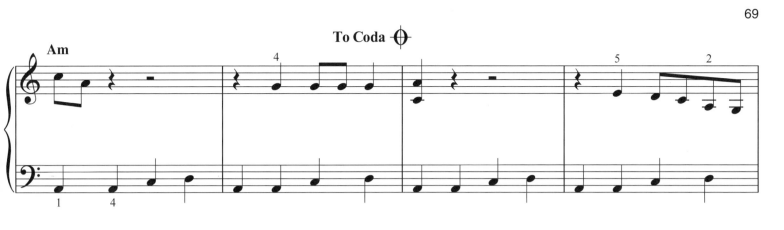

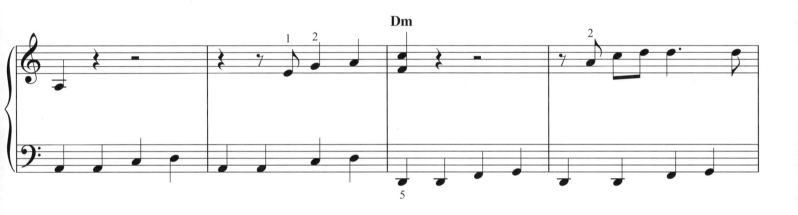

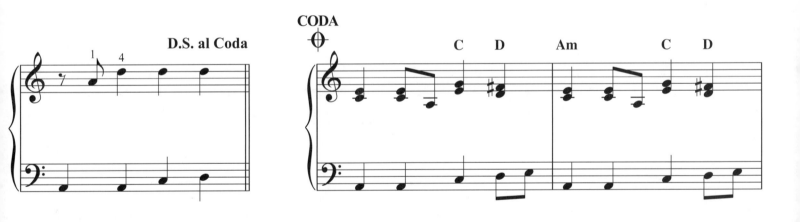

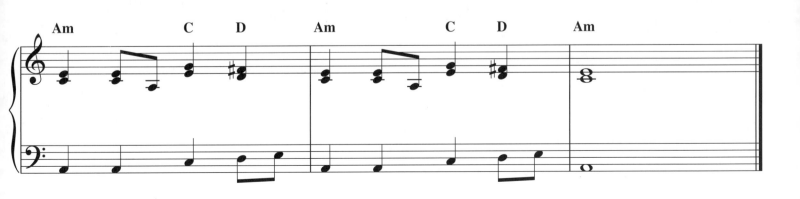

Hallelujah

Electronic Organs
Upper: Flutes (or Tibias) 16', 8', 4'
Lower: Melodia 8', Reed 8'
Pedal: 8'
Vib./Trem.: On, Fast

Drawbar Organs
Upper: 80 4800 000
Lower: (00) 7334 011
Pedal: 05
Vib./Trem.: On, Fast

Words and Music by
Leonard Cohen

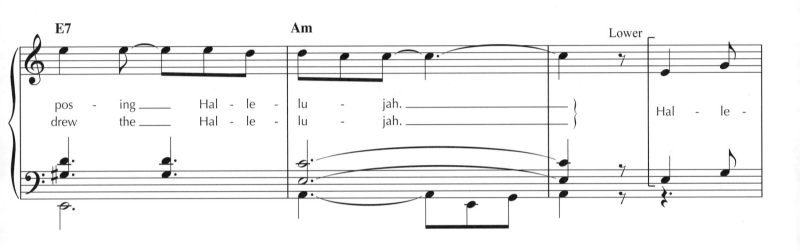

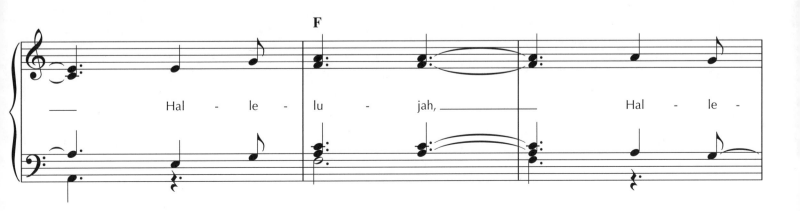

74

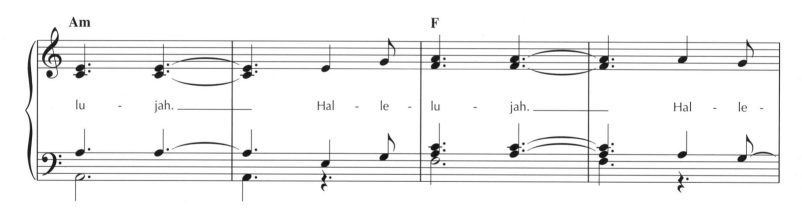

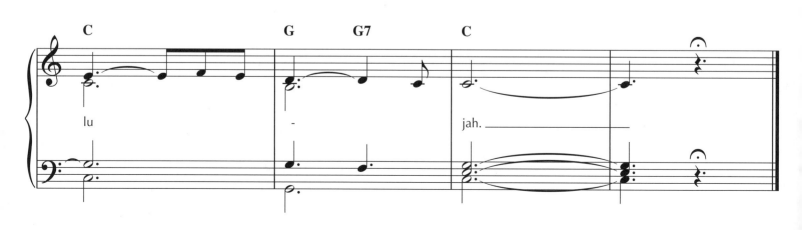

Imagine

Electronic Organs

Upper: Flutes (or Tibias) 8', 5 1/3', 4'
Lower: Strings 4', Piano
Pedal: 16', 8'
Vib./Trem.: On, Slow

Drawbar Organs

Upper: 40 0006 010
Lower: (00) 4004 000 and/or Piano
Pedal: 34
Vib./Trem.: On, Slow

Words and Music by
John Lennon

76

Hallelujah Chorus
from MESSIAH

Electronic Organs

Upper: Full Organ 16', 8', 4',
   2', 1' Brassy, Brilliant
   (or Strings 8', 4', Reeds
   8', 4')
Lower: Flutes 8', 4', Diapason 8',
   Strings 8', 4'
Pedal: 16', 8"Sustain
Vib./Trem.: On, Full (Opt. Off)

Tonebar Organ

Upper: 60 8858 777
Lower: (00) 6555 555
Pedal: 62 Sustain
Vib./Trem.: On, Full (Opt. Off)

By George Frideric Handel

House of the Rising Sun

Electronic Organs
Upper: Flutes 8', 4'
Lower: Strings
Pedal: Bass 8', 16'
      or Elec. bass (soft)
Vib./Trem.: Off

Drawbar Organs
Upper: 60 0608 008
Lower: (00) 6500 001
Pedal: 05
Vib./Trem.: Off

Southern American Folksong

And it's been the ruin of

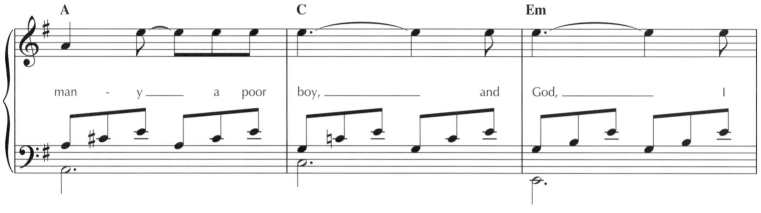

man - y a poor boy, and God, I

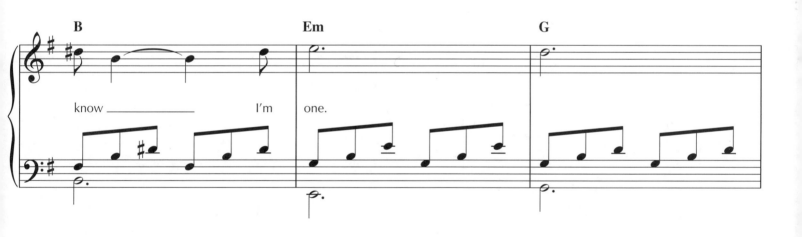

know I'm one.

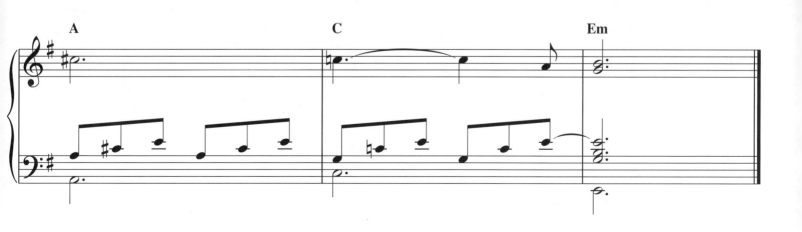

I Dreamed a Dream
from LES MISÉRABLES

Electronic Organs
Upper: Clarinet 8'
Lower: Flutes 8', 4'
Pedal: 16', 8'
Vib./Trem.: On, Fast

Drawbar Organs
Upper: 80 8800 001
Lower: (00) 8404 003
Pedal: 34
Vib./Trem.: On, Fast

Music by Claude-Michel Schönberg
Lyrics by Alain Boublil, Jean-Marc Natel
and Herbert Kretzmer

It's a Small World

from Disney Parks' "it's a small world" attraction

Electronic and Pipe Organs

Upper: Trumpet (or Brass) 8'
Lower: Flutes 8', 4', String 8', Reed 4'
Pedal: 16', 8' Sustain
Trem: On — Full
Automatic Rhythm: March

Drawbar Organs

Upper: 00 6787 654 (00)
Lower: (00) 7654 332 (0)
Pedal: 5 (0) 5 (0) (Spinet 5)
String Bass
Vibrato: On — Full
Automatic Rhythm: March

Words and Music by RICHARD M. SHERMAN
and ROBERT B. SHERMAN

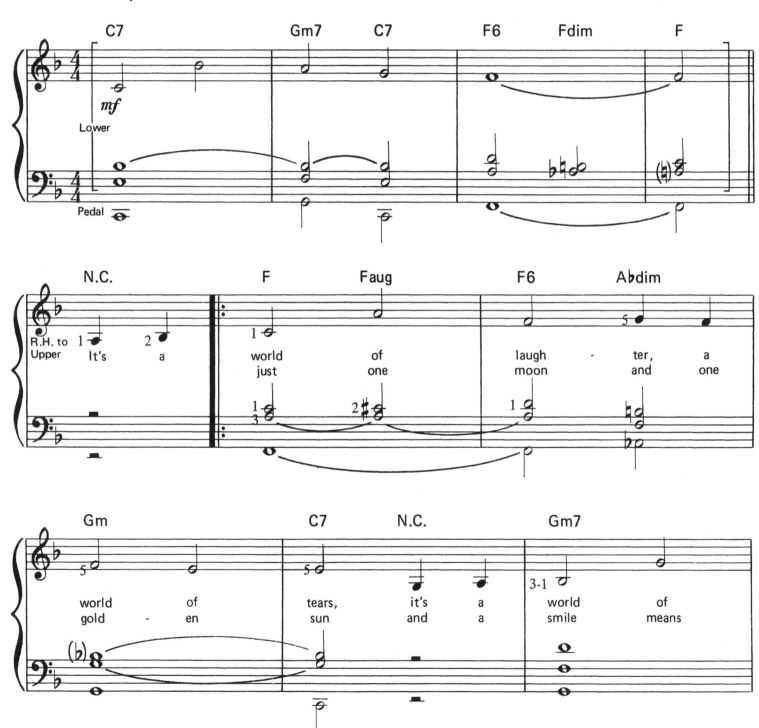

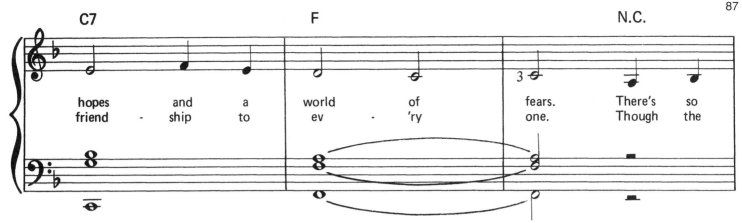

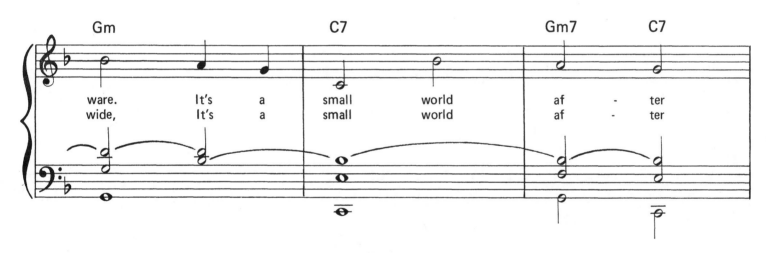

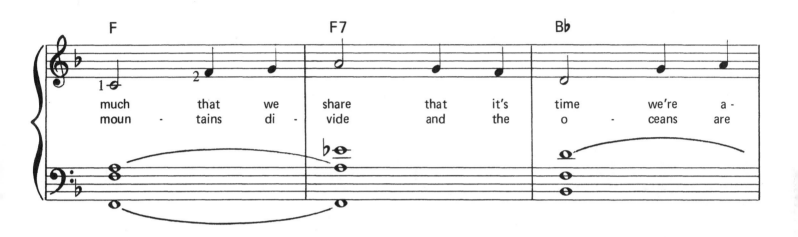

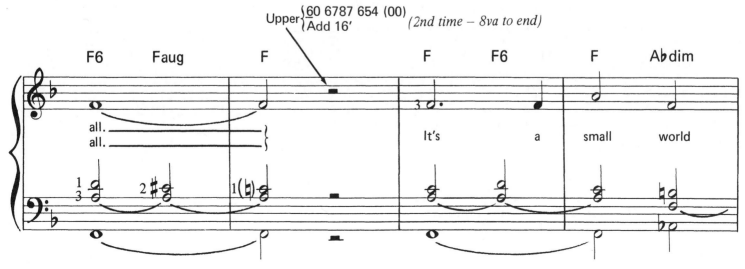

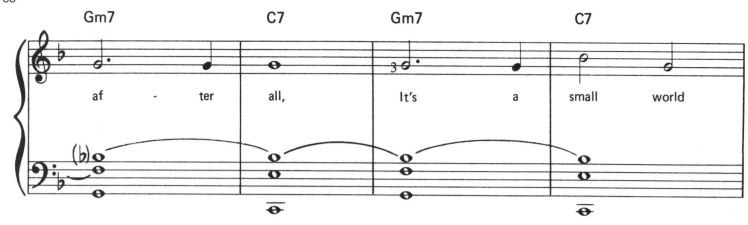

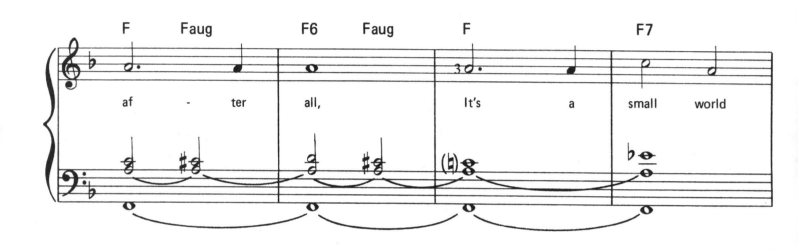

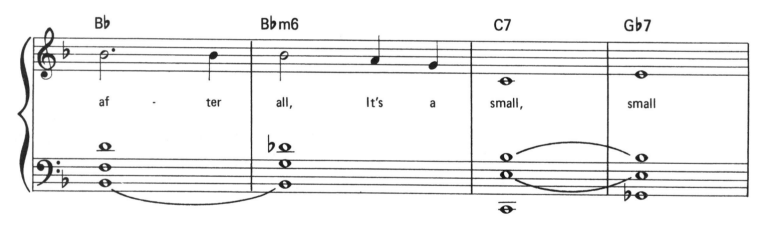

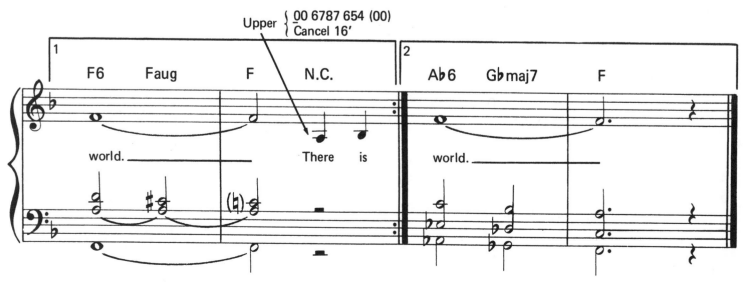

Let It Be

Electronic Organs
Upper: Flutes (or Tibias) 16', 8', 4'
Lower: Melodia 8', Reed 8'
Pedal: 8'
Vib./Trem.: On, Fast

Tonebar Organs
Upper: 80 4800 000
Lower: (00) 7334 011
Pedal: 05
Vib./Trem.: On, Fast

Words and Music by John Lennon
and Paul McCartney

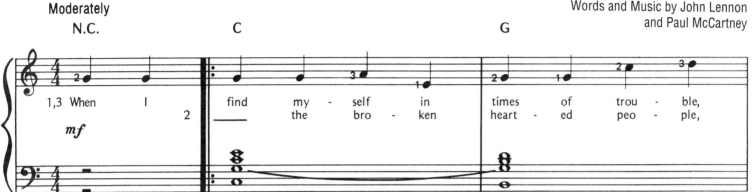

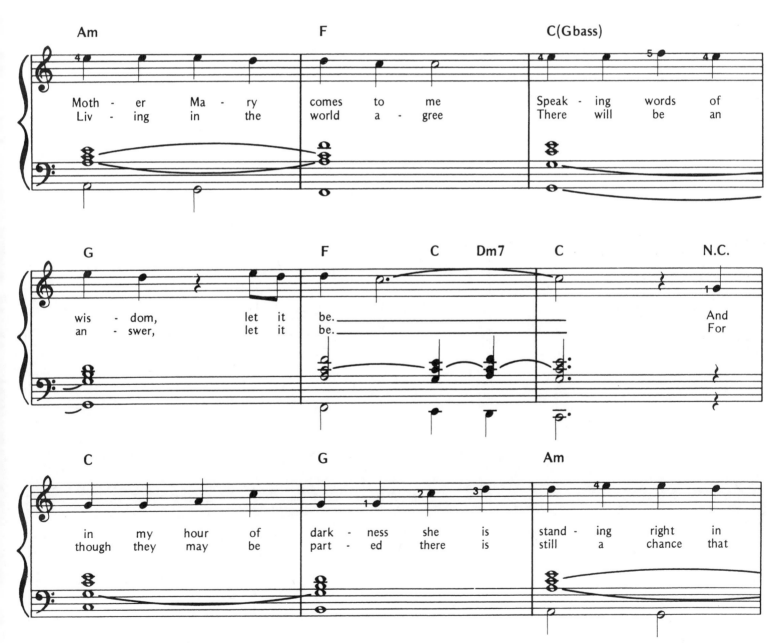

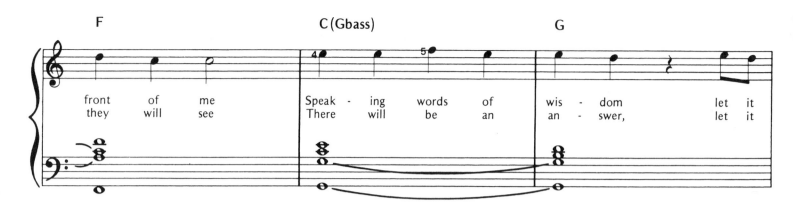

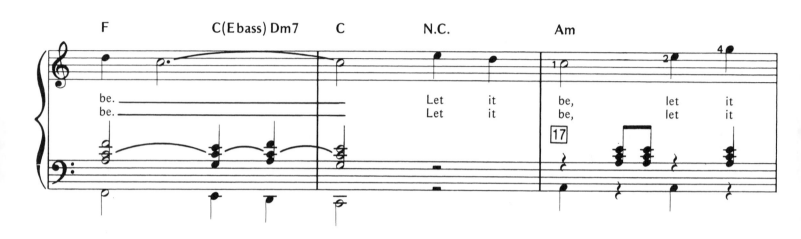

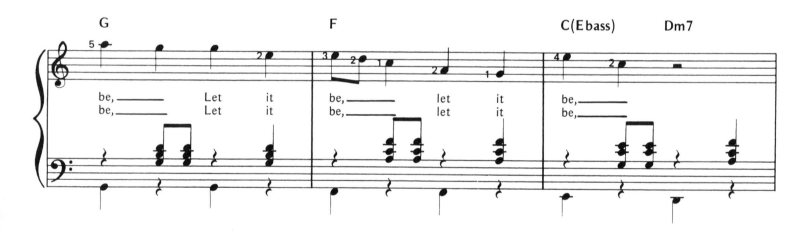

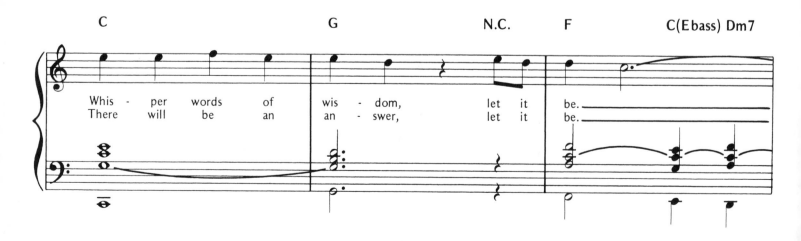

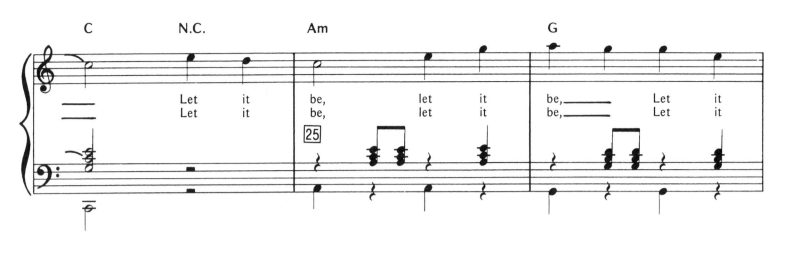

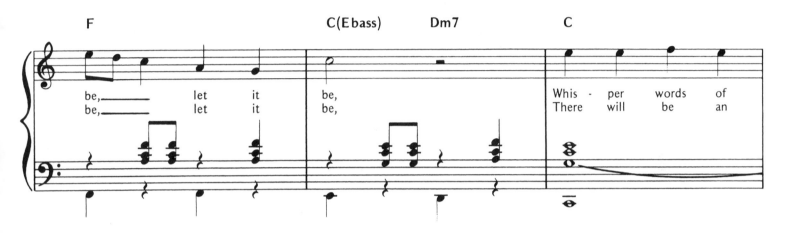

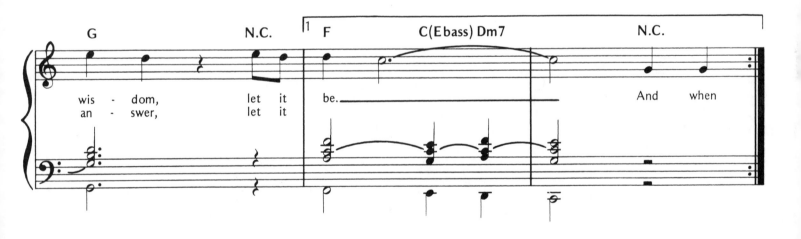

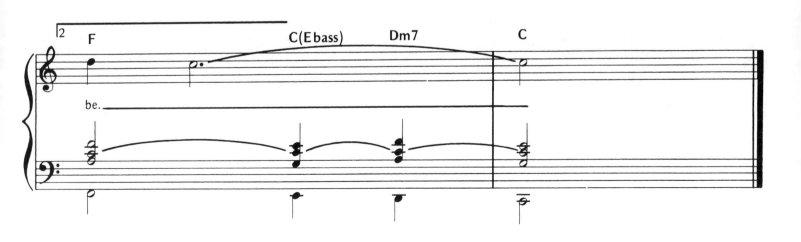

Love Me Tender

Electronic Organs
Upper: Flute (or Tibia) 16',
        Clarinet 8'
Lower: Flutes 8', 4', String 4'
Pedal: 16', 8' Sustain
Vib./Trem.: On Full

Drawbar Organs
Upper: 60 8080 806
Lower: (00) 7654 321
Pedal: 55 Sustain
Vib./Trem.: On, Full

Words and Music by Elvis Presley
and Vera Matson

Slowly, with expression

Love me ten - der,   love me sweet;
Love me ten - der,   love me long;

Nev - er   let   me   go.   You   have   made   my
Take   me   to   your   heart.   For   it's   there   that

life   com - plete,   And   I   love   you   so.}
I   be - long,   And   we'll   nev - er   part.}

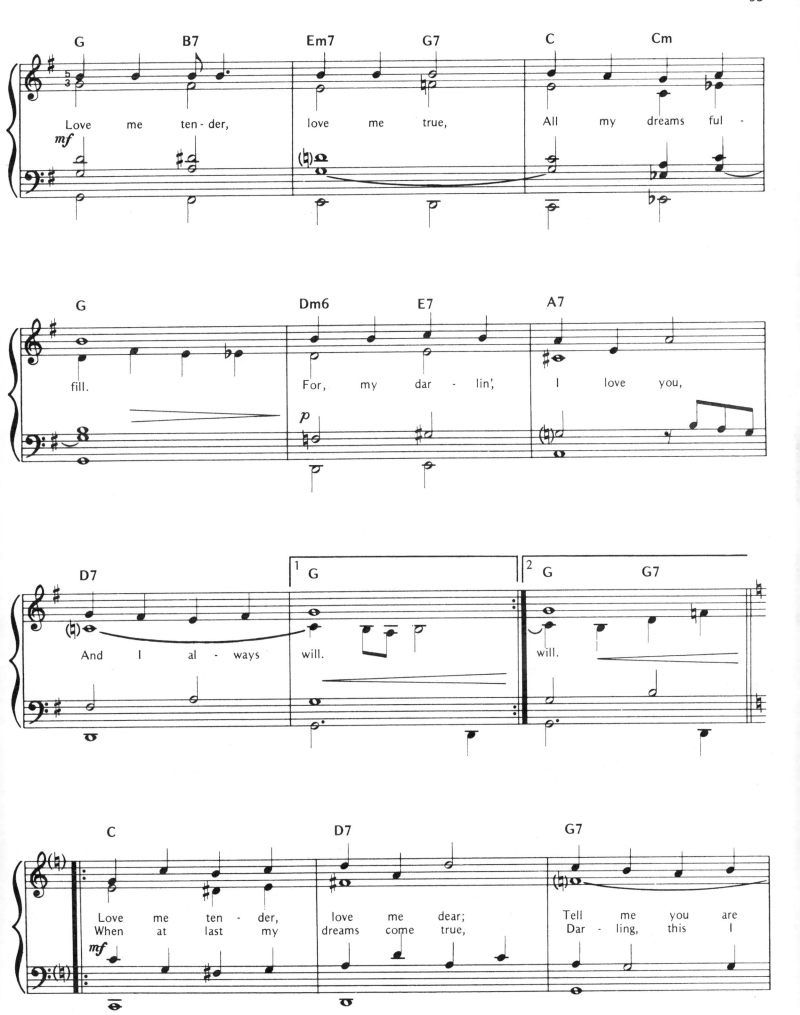

More
(Ti guarderò nel cuore)
from the film MONDO CANE

Electronic Organs
Upper: Flutes (or Tibias) 16′, 8′, 4′, 2′
      Strings 8′, 4′, Trumpet
Lower: Flutes 8′, 4′, Strings 8′, 4′
      Reed 8′
Pedal: 16′, 8′
Vib./Trem.: On, Fast

Drawbar Organs
Upper: 80 7105 123
Lower: (00) 7314 003
Pedal: 25
Vib./Trem.: On, Fast

Music by Nino Oliviero and Riz Ortolani
Italian Lyrics by Marcello Ciorciolini
English Lyrics by Norman Newell

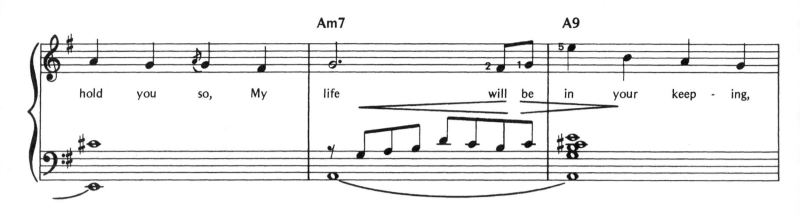

Am7 ... **A9**

hold you so, My life will be in your keep - ing,

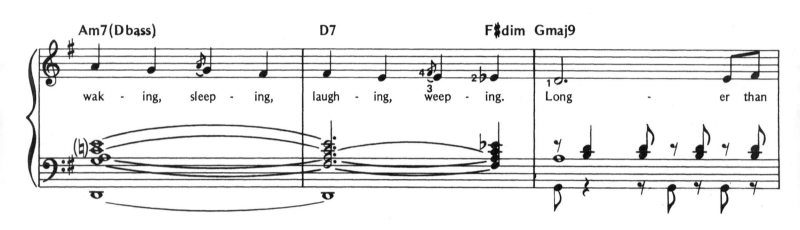

Am7(D bass) ... **D7** ... **F#dim Gmaj9**

wak - ing, sleep - ing, laugh - ing, weep - ing. Long - er than

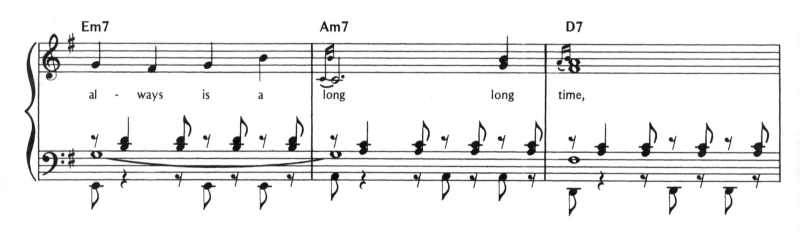

Em7 ... **Am7** ... **D7**

al - ways is a long long time,

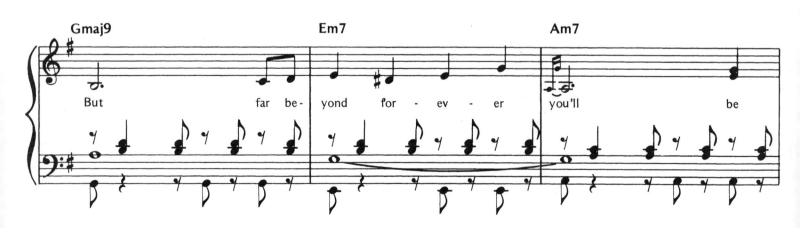

Gmaj9 ... **Em7** ... **Am7**

But far be - yond for - ev - er you'll be

Electronic Organs
Upper: Flutes (or Tibias) 8', 4', 2'
      Strings 8'
      Clarinet
Lower: Flutes 8', 4'
Ped.: 16', 8'
Vib./Trem.: On, Slow

Memory
from CATS

Drawbar Organs
Upper: 30 8104 103
Lower: (00) 6303 004
Ped.: 25
Vib./Trem.: On, Slow

Music by Andrew Lloyd Webber
Text by Trevor Nunn after T.S. Eliot

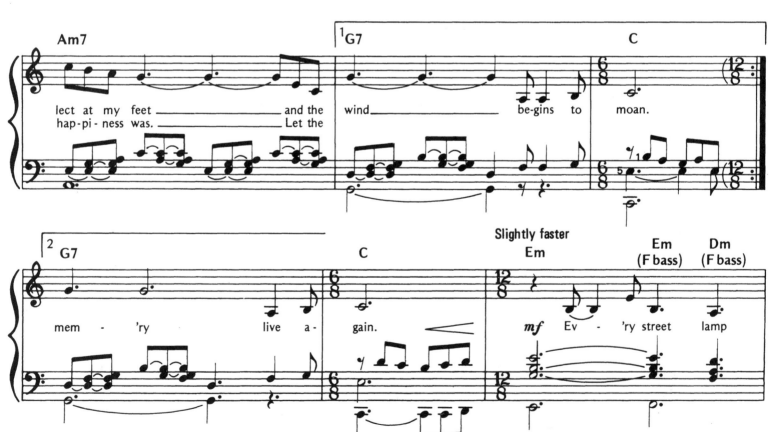

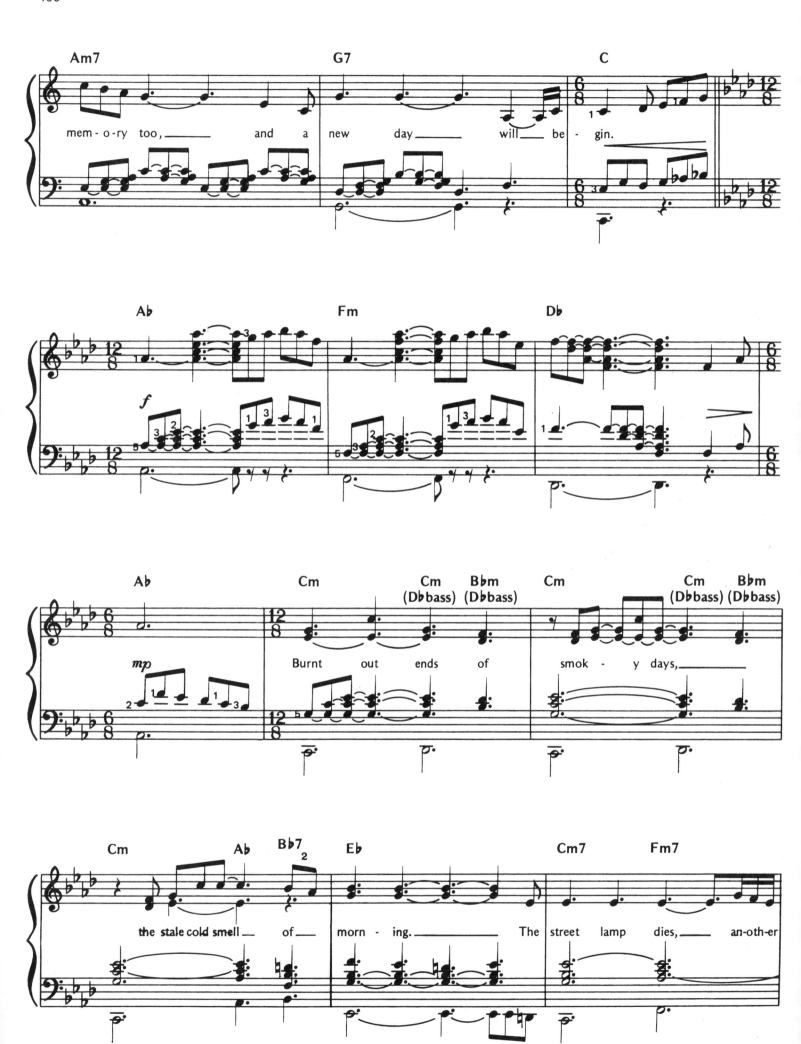

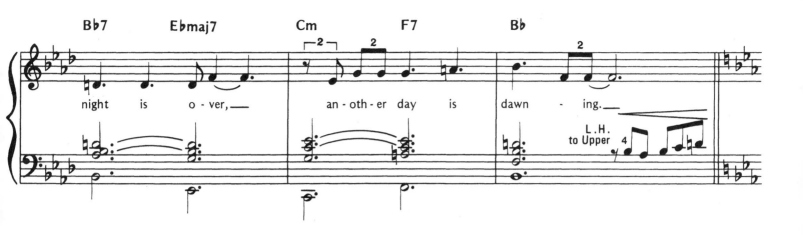

night is o-ver,—— an-oth-er day is dawn - ing.——

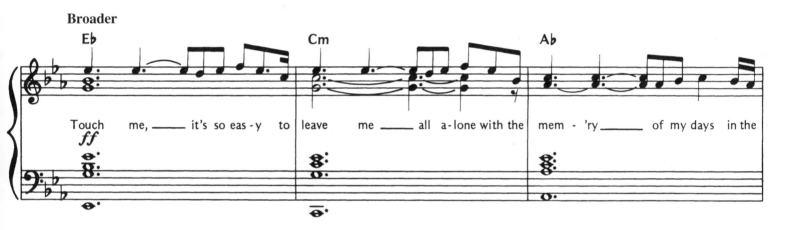

Broader

Touch me,—— it's so eas-y to leave me —— all a-lone with the mem - 'ry—— of my days in the

sun. —— If you touch me, you'll un-der-stand what hap-pi-ness is. Look, a new day has be-

Slowing to end

gun.

A Mighty Fortress Is Our God

Electronic and Pipe Organs

Upper: Full, with 16' and soft reed(s)
Lower: Full, with 16' and soft reed(s) (all couplers)
Pedal: *ff* 16' and 8' with Op. Diapason(s) and soft
       reed(s) (all couplers)

Drawbar Organs

Upper: 56 8888 765 (54)
Lower: (44) 8888 7655 (5)
Pedal: 8 (0) 6 (0) (Spinet 8)

Words and Music by Martin Luther
Based on Psalm 46

*Set stops and drawbars at "full organ" for ending phrase.

On My Own
from LES MISÉRABLES

Electronic Organs
Upper: Clarinet 8'
Lower: Flutes 8', 4', String 4'
Pedal: 16',8'
Vib./Trem.: On, Fast

Drawbar Organs
Upper: 80 8800 001
Lower: (00) 7345 012
Pedal: 34
Vib./Trem.: On, Fast

Music by Claude-Michel Schönberg
Lyrics by Alain Boublil, Jean-Marc Natel,
Herbert Kretzmer, John Caird
and Trevor Nunn

The Phantom of the Opera
from THE PHANTOM OF THE OPERA

Electronic Organs
Upper: Flutes (or Tibias) 16', 8', 5-1/3', 4'
Lower: Pipe Organ
Pedal: String Bass
Vib./Trem.: On, Slow

Drawbar Organs
Upper: 42 0026 010
Lower: Pipe Organ
Pedal: String Bass
Vib./Trem.: On, Slow

Music by Andrew Lloyd Webber
Lyrics by Charles Hart
Additional Lyrics by Richard Stilgoe and Mike Batt

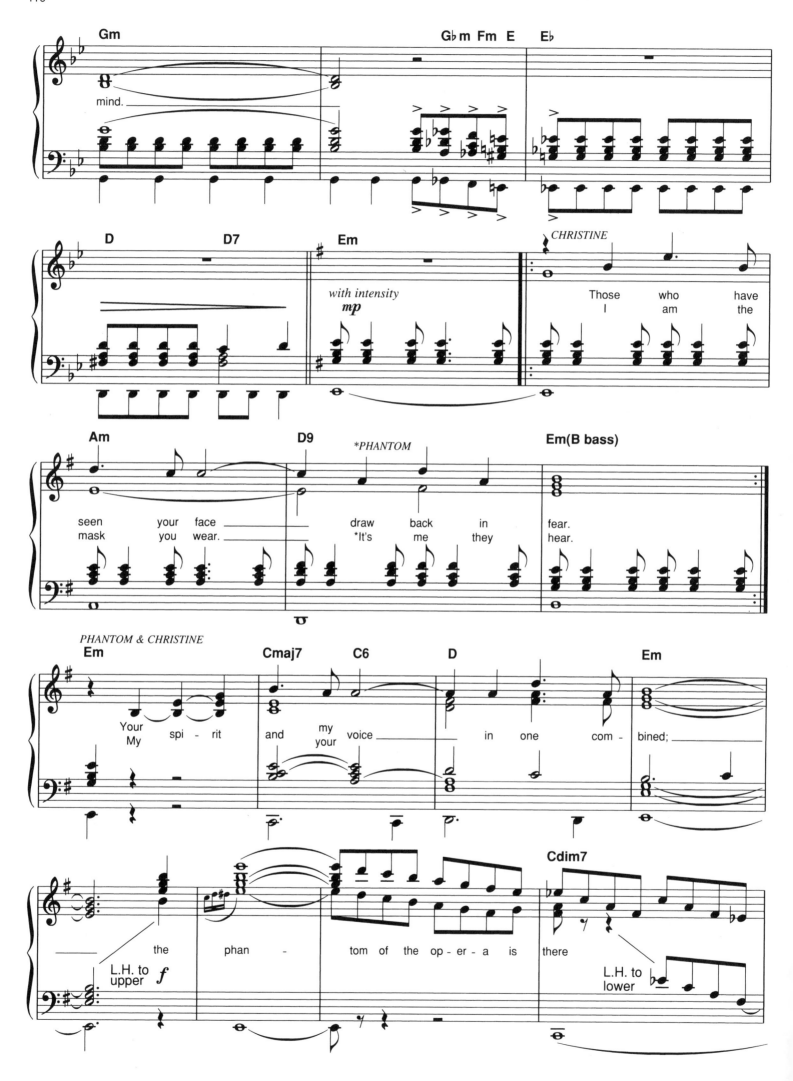

Perfect

Electronic Organs
Upper: Flutes (or Tibias) 8', 2'
        Strings 8', 4'
Lower: Flutes 8', 4'
        Strings 8', 4'
Pedal: 16', 8'
Vib./Trem.: On, Fast

Drawbar Organs
Upper: 82 5325 004
Lower: (00) 7345 312
Pedal: 44
Vib./Trem.: On, Fast

Words and Music by
Ed Sheeran

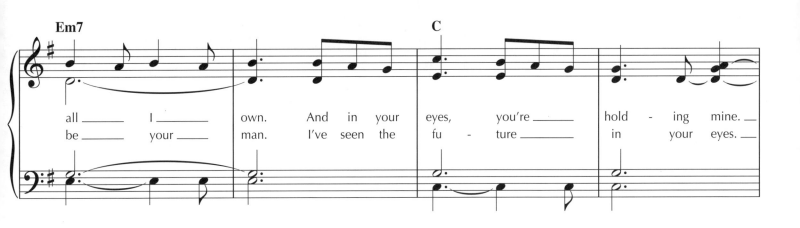

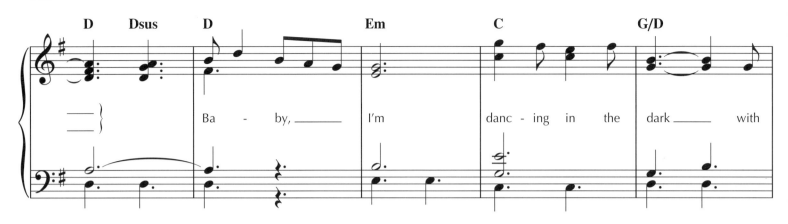

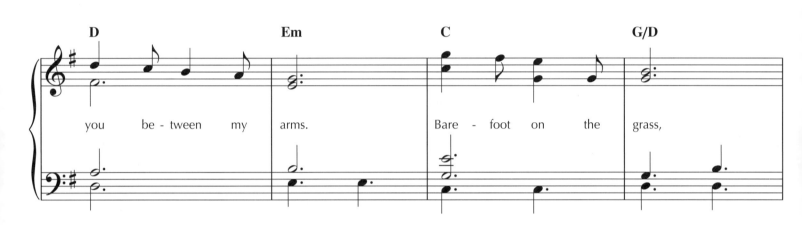

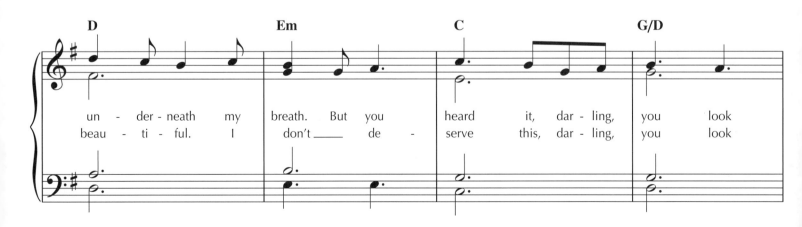

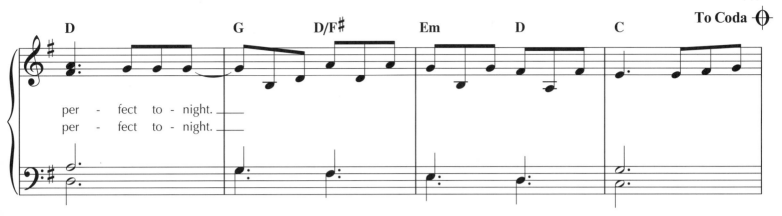

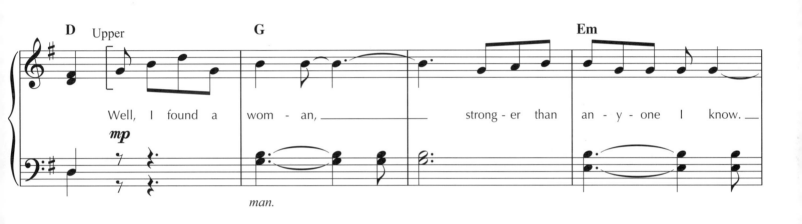

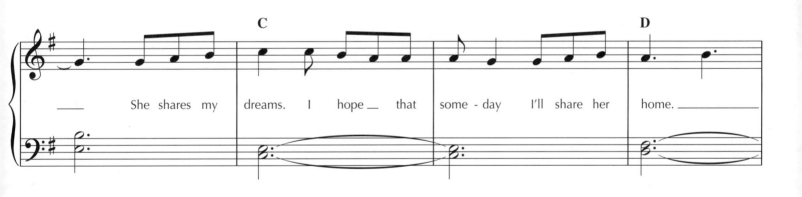

se - crets, to car - ry love, to car - ry chil - dren ___ of our own. ___

D.S. al Coda

Lower

We are still kids, but we're

mf

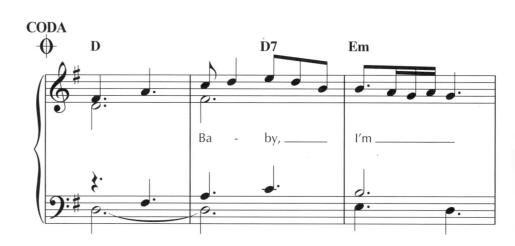

CODA

Ba - by, ___ I'm ___

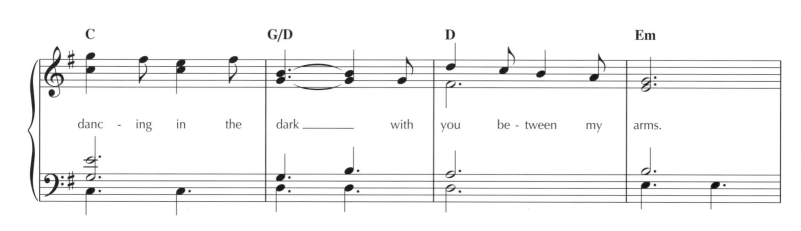

danc - ing in the dark ___ with you be - tween my arms.

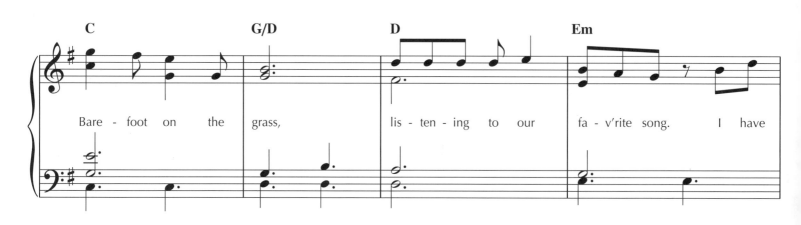

Bare - foot on the grass, lis - ten - ing to our fa - v'rite song. I have

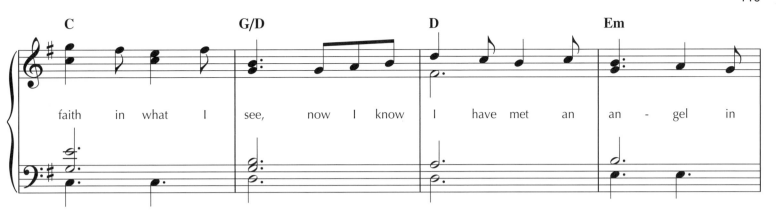

faith in what I see, now I know I have met an an - gel in

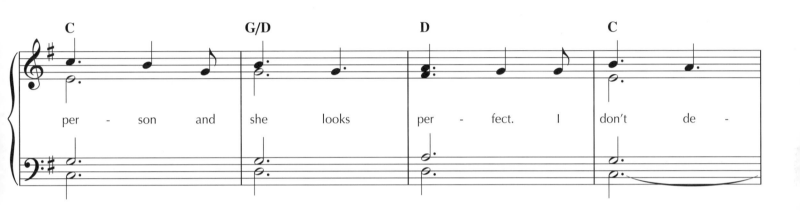

per - son and she looks per - fect. I don't de -

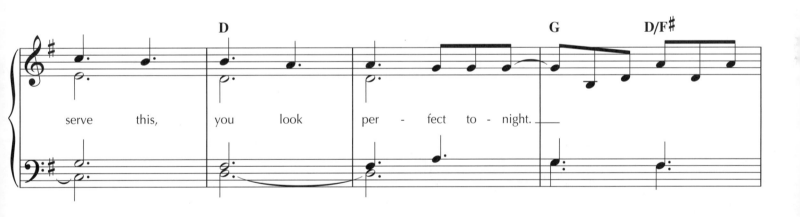

serve this, you look per - fect to - night.

Rock of Ages

Electronic and Pipe Organs

Upper: Fr. Horn (Fl.) 8'
Lower: Stgs. 8', 4'
Pedal: Soft 16' to Gt.

Drawbar Organs

Upper: 00 8850 000 (00)
Lower: (00) 6116 432 (0)
Pedal: 4 (0) 2 (0) (Spinet 3)

Words by Augustus M. Toplady
Music by Thomas Hastings

September Song
from the Musical Play KNICKERBOCKER HOLIDAY

Electronic Organs
Upper: Flute (or Tibia) 4'
       Clarinet 8'
Lower: Strings 8', 4'
Pedal: 16', 8'
Vib./Trem.: On, Fast

Drawbar Organs
Upper: 53 5864 101
Lower: (00) 7104 000
Pedal: 35
Vib./Trem.: On, Fast

Words by Maxwell Anderson
Music by Kurt Weill

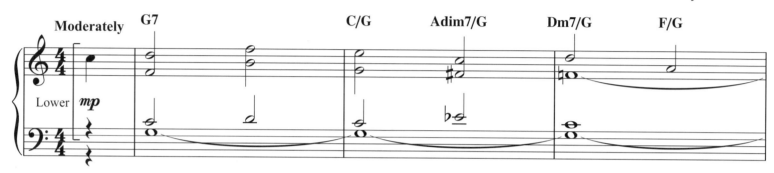

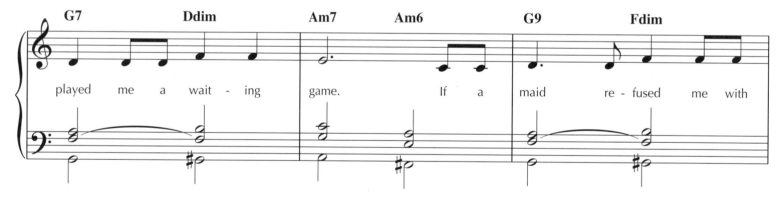

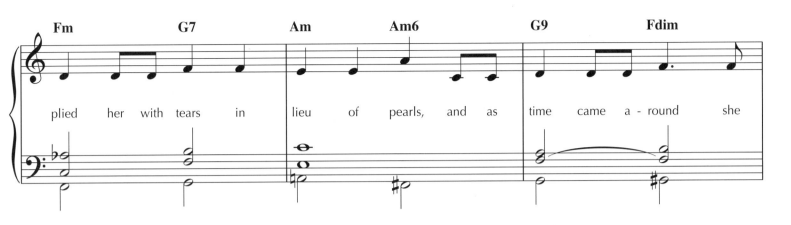

plied her with tears in lieu of pearls, and as time came a - round she

came my way, as time came a - round she came. Oh, it's a

long, long while ___ from May to De - cem - ber, ___

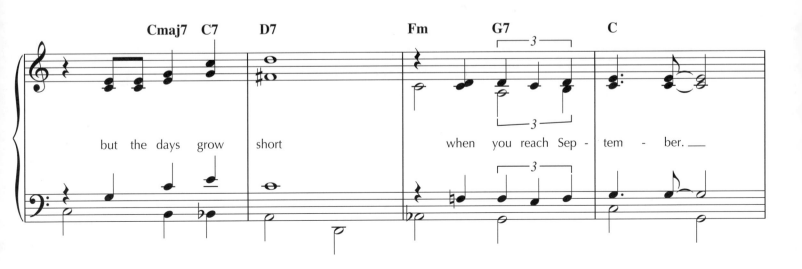

but the days grow short when you reach Sep - tem - ber. ___

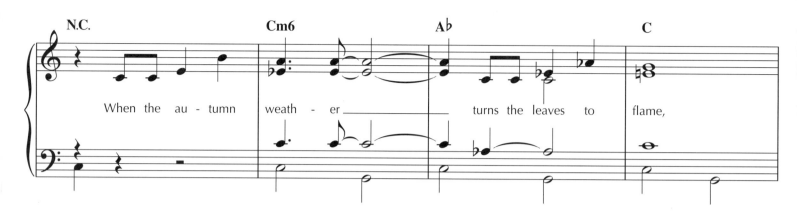

When the au - tumn weath - er _____ turns the leaves to flame,

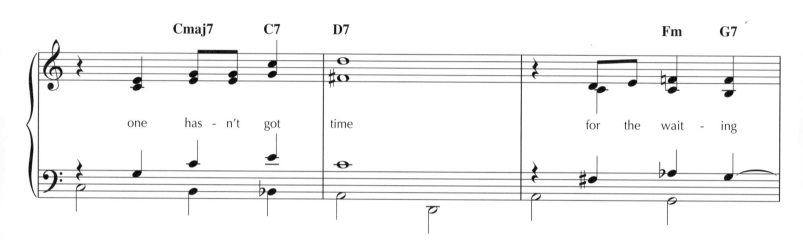

one has - n't got time _____ for the wait - ing

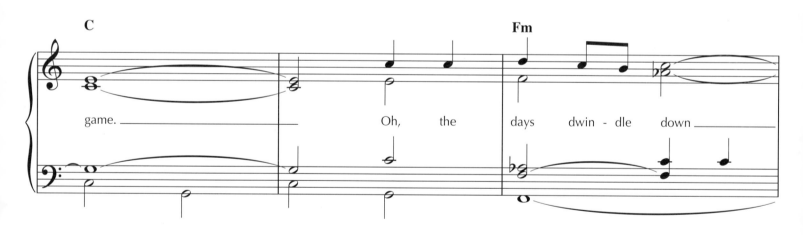

game. _____ Oh, the days dwin - dle down _____

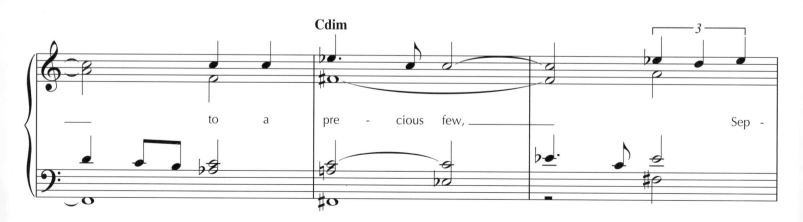

to a pre - cious few, _____ Sep -

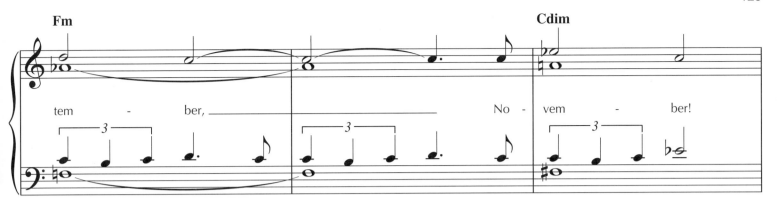

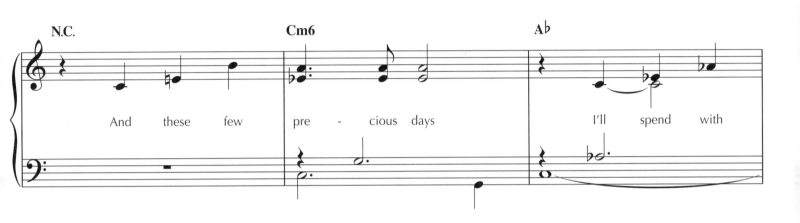

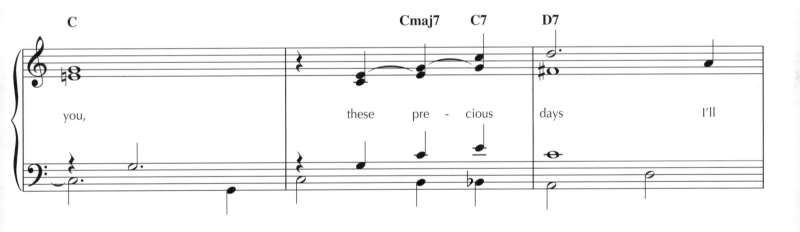

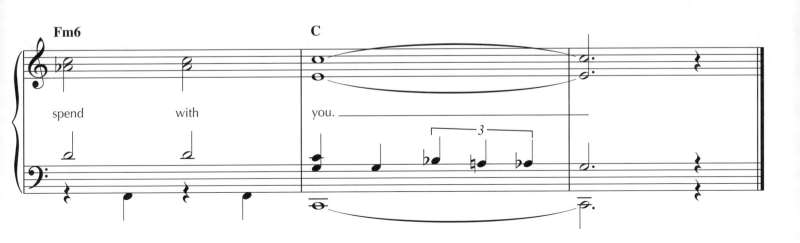

Electronic Organs
Upper: Flutes (or Tibias) 16′, 4′
        Trombone, Trumpet
Lower: Flute 8′, Diapason 8′, Reed 8′
Pedal: 8′
Vib./Trem.: On, Fast

Stardust

Drawbar Organs
Upper: 82 5864 200
Lower: (00) 7103 000
Pedal: 04
Vib./Trem.: On, Fast

Words by Mitchell Parish
Music by Hoagy Carmichael

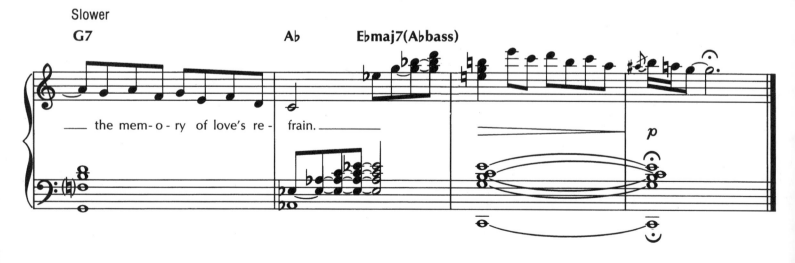

Sunrise, Sunset
from the Musical FIDDLER ON THE ROOF

Electronic Organs
Upper: Flute (or Tibia) 4', Oboe 8'
Lower: Flute 8', String 8'
Pedal: 8'
Vib./Trem.: On, Fast

Drawbar Organs
Upper: 00 6640 000
Lower: (00) 5323 001
Pedal: 34
Vib./Trem.: On, Fast

Words by Sheldon Harnick
Music by Jerry Bock

Supercalifragilisticexpialidocious

from Walt Disney's MARY POPPINS

Electronic and Pipe Organs

Upper: Flutes (or Tibias) 16', 4', 1'
Lower: Diapason 8'
       String 4'
Pedal: 16', 8' Sustain
Trem: On — Full
Automatic Rhythm: Swing

Drawbar Organs

Upper: 60 0800 008 (00)
Lower: (00) 5433 323 (0)
Pedal: 5 (0) 5 (0) (Spinet 5)
      String Bass
Vibrato: On — Full
Automatic Rhythm: Swing

Words and Music by RICHARD M. SHERMAN
and ROBERT B. SHERMAN

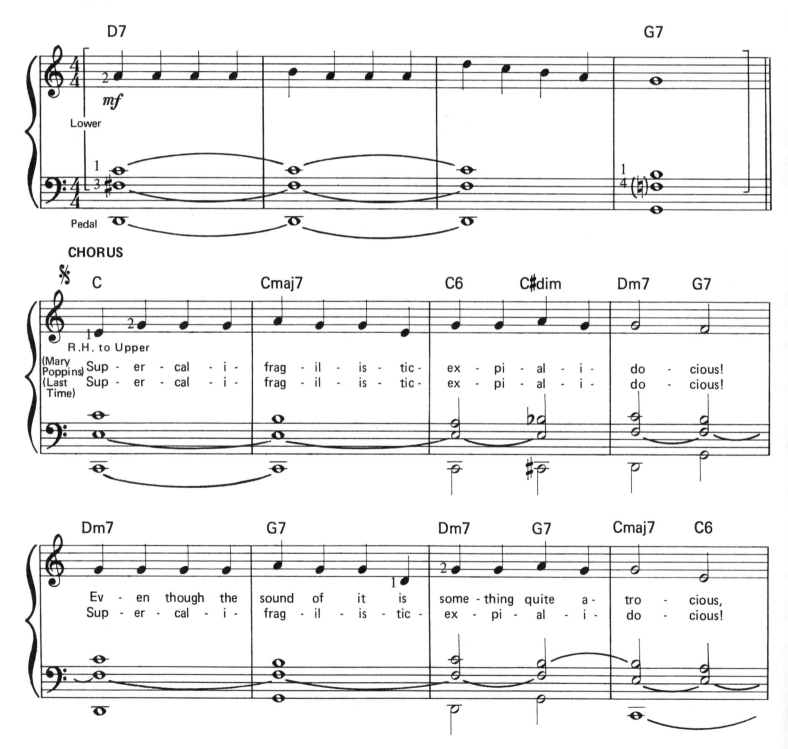

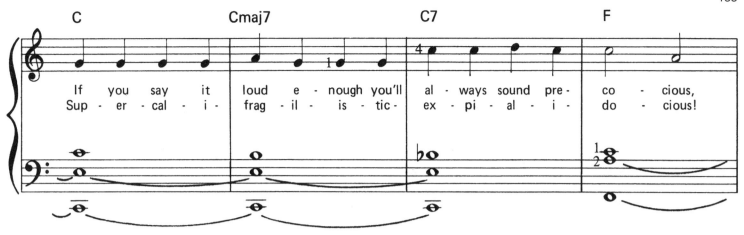

If you say it loud e - nough you'll al - ways sound pre - co - cious,
Sup - er - cal - i - frag - il - is - tic - ex - pi - al - i - do - cious!

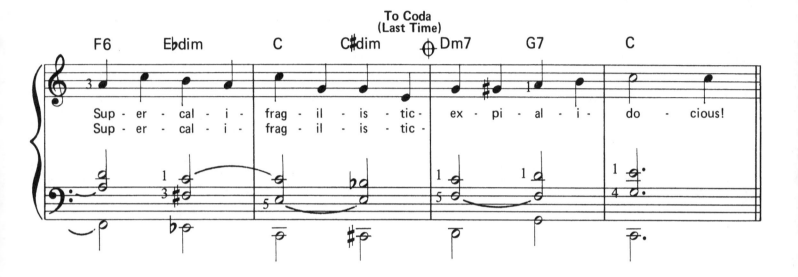

To Coda
(Last Time)

Sup - er - cal - i - frag - il - is - tic - ex - pi - al - i - do - cious!
Sup - er - cal - i - frag - il - is - tic -

VERSE

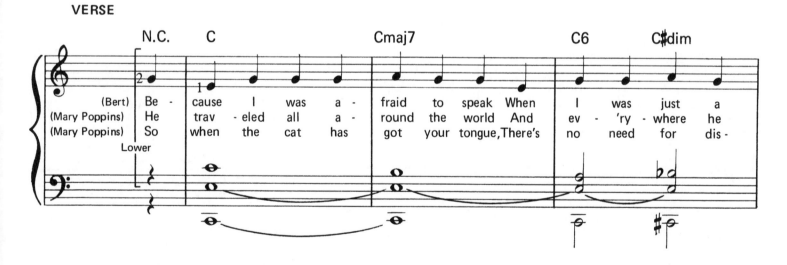

(Bert) Be - cause I was a - fraid to speak When I was just a
(Mary Poppins) He trav - eled all a - round the world And ev - 'ry - where he
(Mary Poppins) So when the cat has got your tongue, There's no need for dis -

Lower

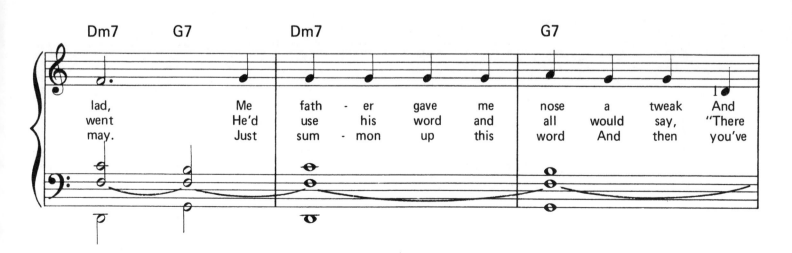

lad, Me fath - er gave me nose a tweak And
went He'd use his word and all would say, "There
may. Just sum - mon up this word And then you've

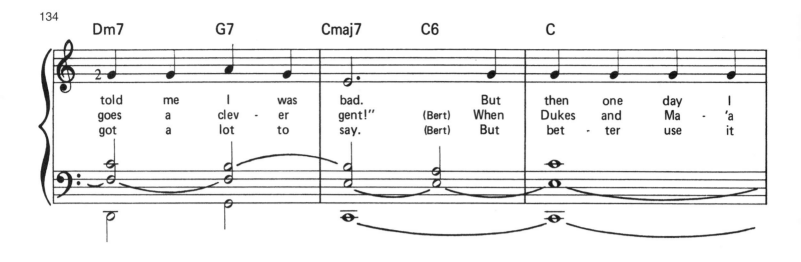

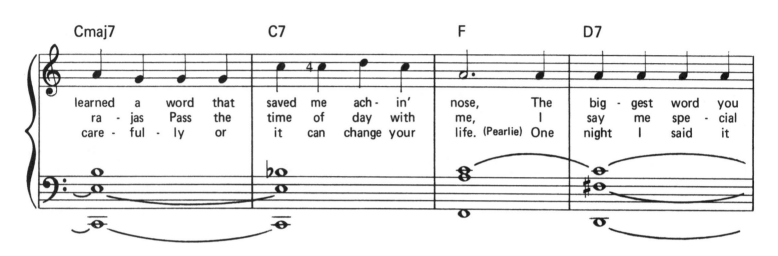

✛ **CODA**

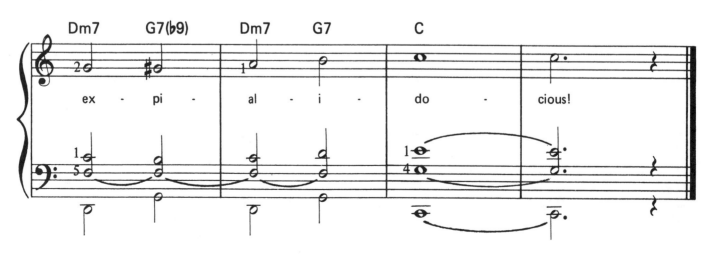

Think of Me
from THE PHANTOM OF THE OPERA

Electronic Organs
Upper: Flutes (or Tibias) 16', 4'
Lower: String 8', Reed 4'
Pedal: 16', 8'
Vib./Trem.: On, Fast

Drawbar Organs
Upper: 80 0800 000
Lower: (00) 4004 010
Pedal: 24
Vib./Trem.: On, Fast
Music by Andrew Lloyd Webber
Lyrics by Charles Hart
Additional Lyrics by Richard Stilgoe

Allegretto

This Is Me
from THE GREATEST SHOWMAN

Electronic Organs
Upper: Flutes (or Tibias) 8', 4'
Lower: Diapason 8'
Pedal: 8', 16'
Vib./Trem.: Off

Drawbar Organs
Upper: 00 8300 000
Lower: (00) 6502 000
Pedal: 04
Vib./Trem.: Off

Words and Music by Benj Pasek
and Justin Paul

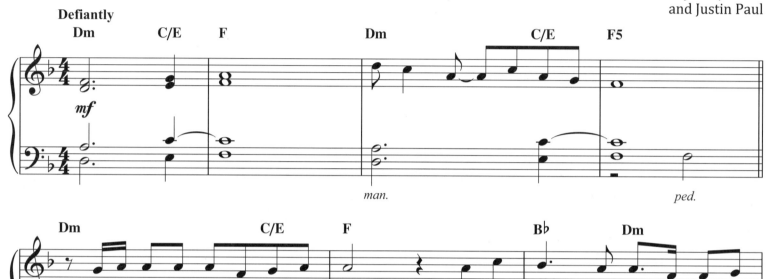

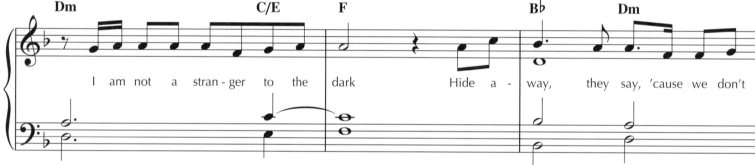

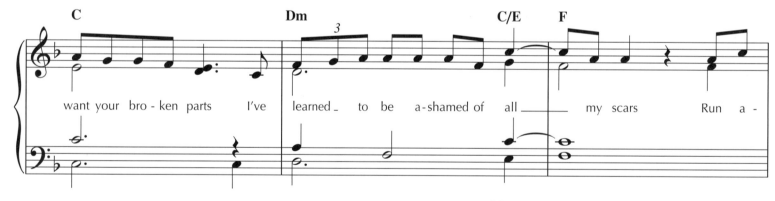

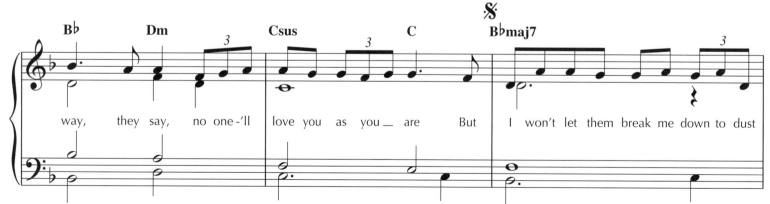

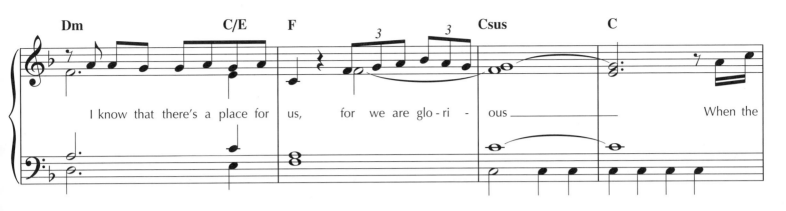

I know that there's a place for us, for we are glo-ri - ous _____ When the

sharp-est words_ wan-na cut me down, _ I'm gon-na send a flood,_ gon-na drown 'em out _

_____ I am brave, I am bruised, I am who ____ I'm meant to be This is me

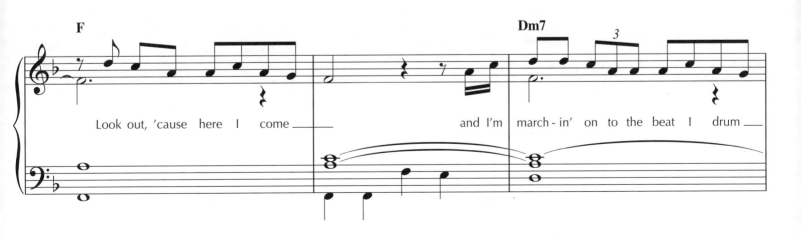

Look out, 'cause here I come _____ and I'm march-in' on to the beat I drum _____

I'm not scared to be seen I make no a-pol-o-gies This is me

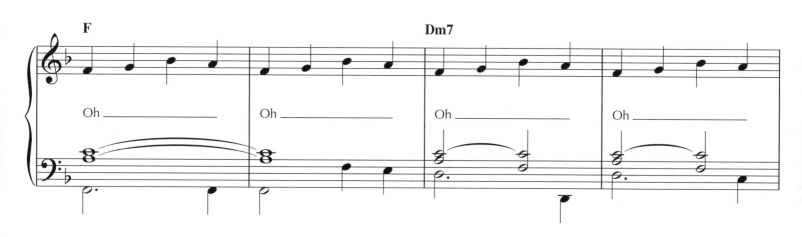

Oh Oh Oh Oh

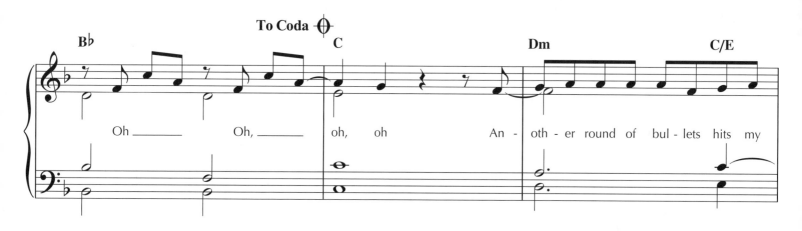

To Coda

Oh Oh, oh, oh An-oth-er round of bul-lets hits my

skin Well, fire a-way, 'cause to-day I won't let the shame sink in We are

burst-in' through the bar - ri - cades and reach-in' for the sun We are war - ri - ors Yeah that's

what we've be - come

CODA

oh, oh This is me Oh

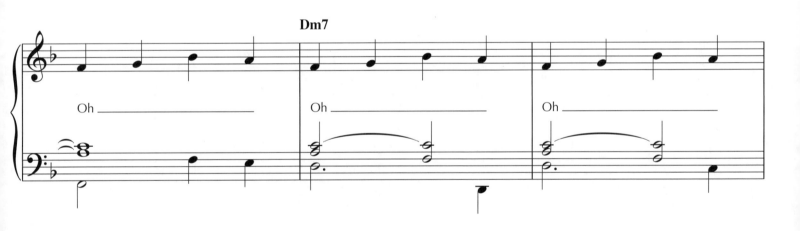

Oh   Oh   Oh

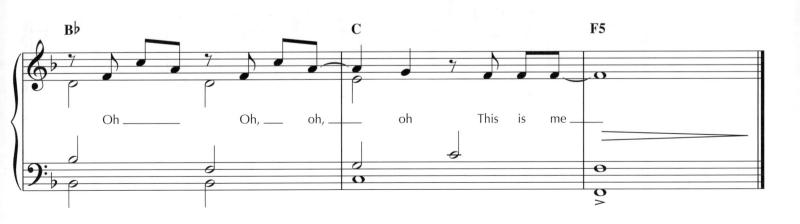

Oh   Oh,   oh,   oh This is me

Trumpet Voluntary

Electronic and Pipe Organs

Upper: Trumpet 8′, Stgs. 8′, Fls. 8′ and 4′
Lower: Horn 8′, Stgs. 8′ and 4′ (Open Diap. 8′ ad lib.)
Pedal: 16′ and 8′ to balance Gt. to Ped.

Drawbar Organs

Upper: 00 8887 650 (00)
Lower: (00) 6665 322 (0)
Pedal: 5 (0) 3 (0) (Spinet 4)

By JEREMIAH CLARKE

*Any of the sections may be repeated if desired.

*This section may be repeated, if desired, an octave higher on the upper ad lib.

Unchained Melody
from the Motion Picture UNCHAINED

Electronic Organs
Upper: Flutes 16', 8', 4'
Lower: Flutes 8', 4'
Pedal: 8'
Vib./Trem.: On, Fast

Drawbar Organs
Upper: 80 4800 000
Lower: (00) 6500 000
Pedal: 05
Vib./Trem.: On, Fast

Lyric by Hy Zaret
Music by Alex North

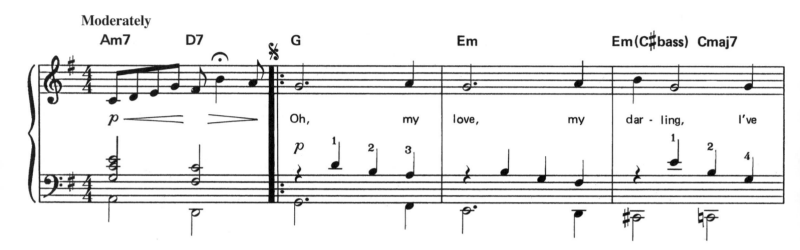

Oh, my love, my dar - ling, I've

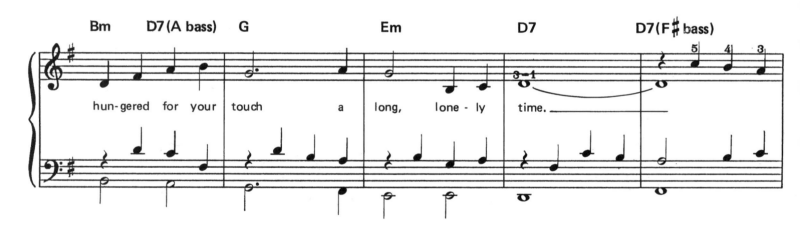

hun-gered for your touch a long, lone - ly time.

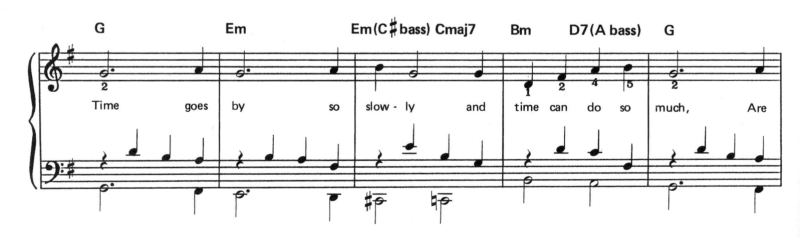

Time goes by so slow - ly and time can do so much, Are

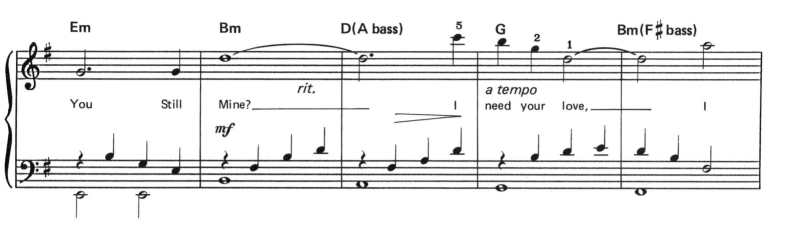

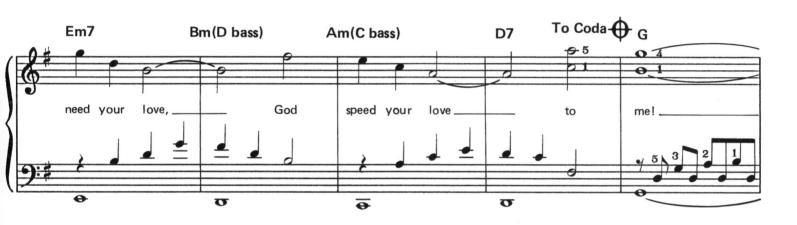

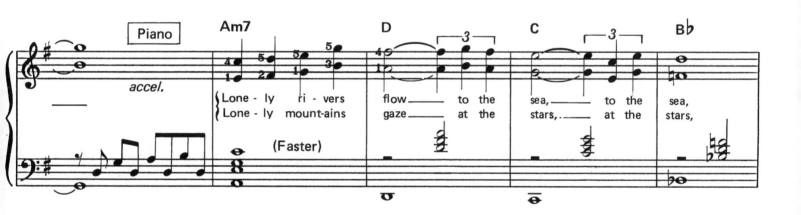

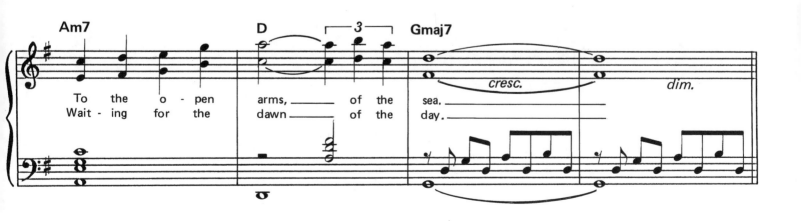

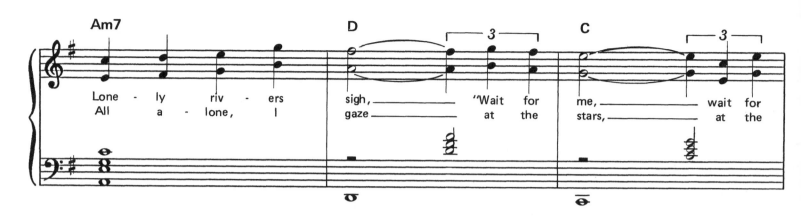

Lone - ly riv - ers sigh, _____ "Wait for me, _____ wait for
All a - lone, I gaze _____ at the stars, _____ at the

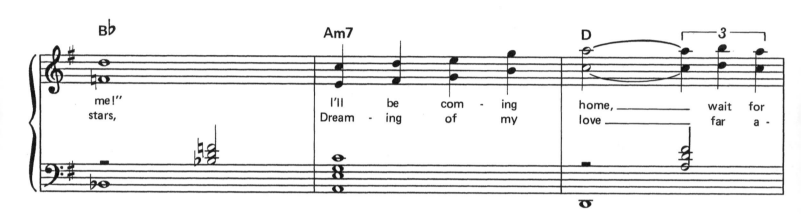

me!" stars,
I'll be com - ing home, _____ wait for
Dream - ing of my love _____ far a -

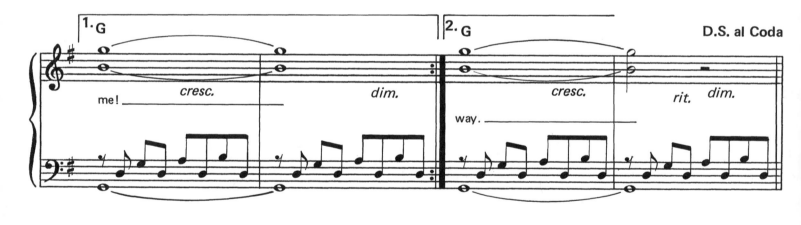

me! _____ cresc. dim.
way. _____ cresc. rit. dim.

D.S. al Coda

CODA

dim. poco a poco rit. poco a poco
me! _____

A Whole New World
from ALADDIN

Electronic Organs
Upper: Oboe 8'
Lower: Piano (Med. sustain)
Pedal: Bass 8'
Vib./Trem.: Off

Drawbar Organs
Upper: 08 00800 002
Lower: Preset Piano or
    (00) 7400 000
Pedals: 25
Vib./Trem.: Off

Music by ALAN MENKEN
Lyrics by TIM RICE

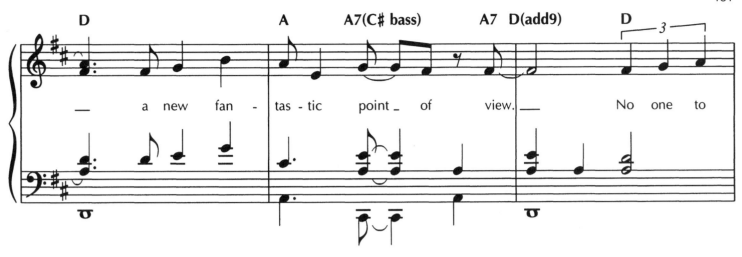

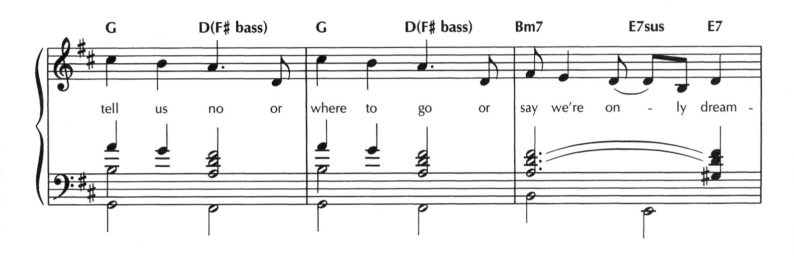

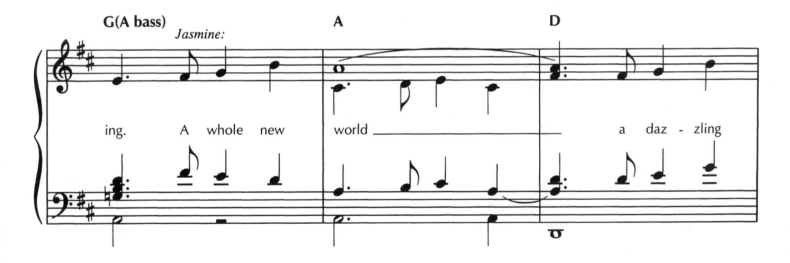

154

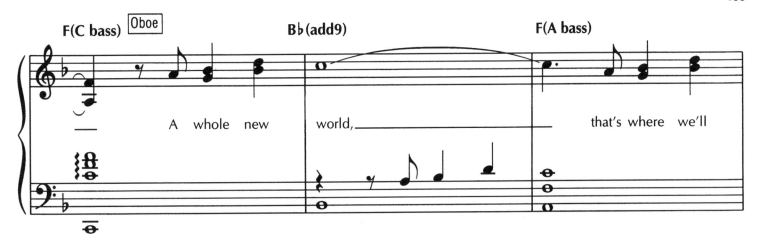

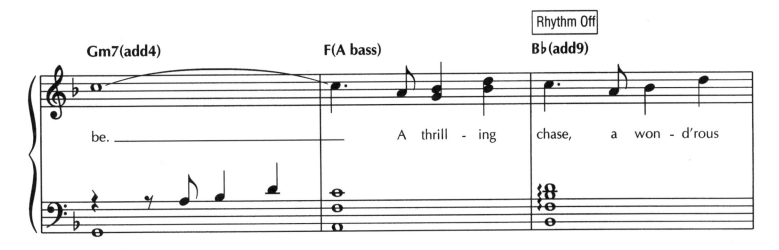

Wedding Processional
from THE SOUND OF MUSIC

Electronic Organs

Upper: Flutes (or Tibias) 16', 8', 4', 2',
      Strings 8', 4', Trumpet
Lower: Flutes 8', 4', Strings 8', 4',
      Reed 8'
Pedal: 16', 8'
Vib./Trem.: Off

Drawbar Organs

Upper: 80 7104 001
Lower: (00) 8512 002
Pedal: 65
Vib./Trem.: Off

Lyrics by OSCAR HAMMERSTEIN II
Music by RICHARD RODGERS

Stately march

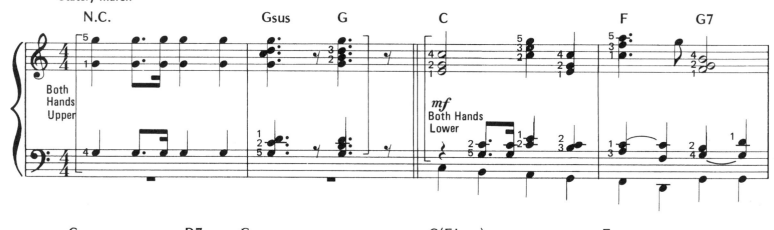

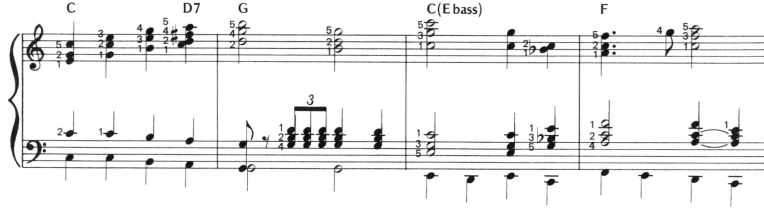

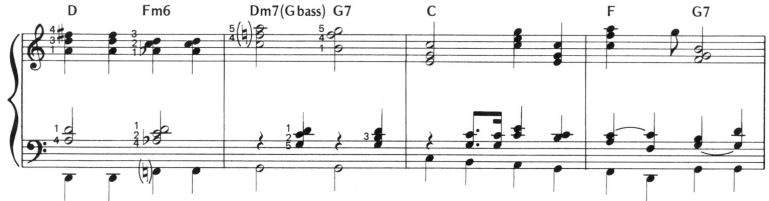

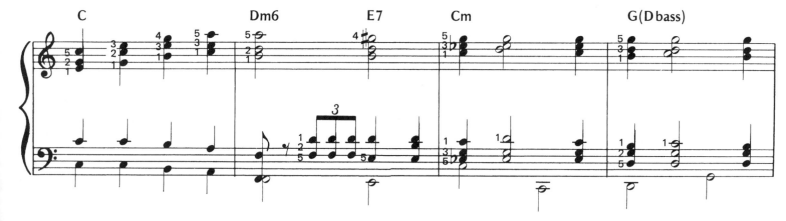

What a Friend We Have in Jesus

Electronic and Pipe Organs

Upper: Fr. Horn (Solo Fl.) 8′
Lower: Stgs. 8′, 4′
Pedal: Soft 16′ to Gt.

Drawbar Organs

Upper: 00 8585 000 (00)
Lower: (00) 5545 321 (0)
Pedal: 4 (0) 2 (0) (Spinet 3)

Words by Joseph M. Scriven
Music by Charles C. Converse

Andante devoto - calmato (M.M. ♩ = 52)

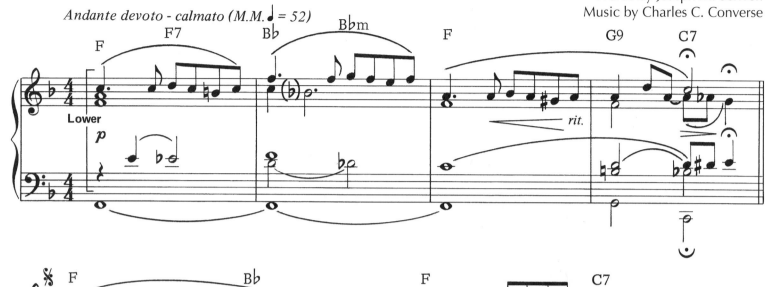

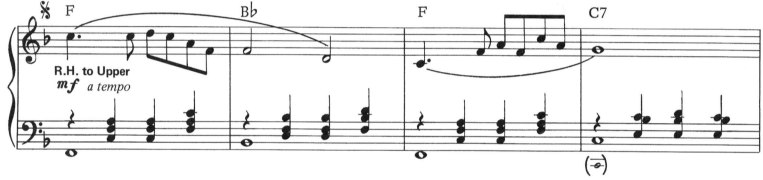

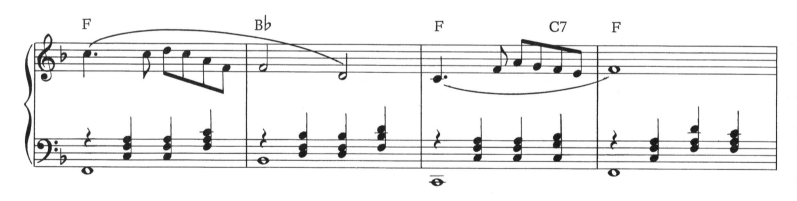

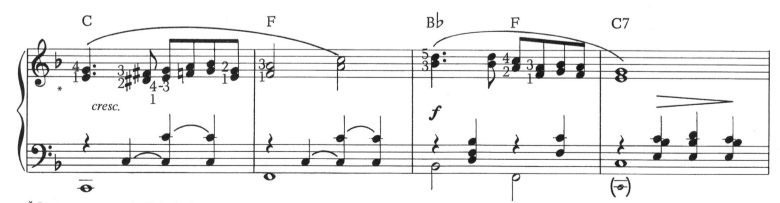

* Play top notes only if desired.

When She Loved Me

from TOY STORY 2

Electronic Organs
Upper: Flute (or Tibia) 4'
       Clarinet 8'
Lower: Strings 8', 4'
Pedal: 16', 8'
Vib./Trem.: On, Fast

Drawbar Organs
Upper: 53 5864 101
Lower: (00) 7104 000
Pedal: 35
Vib./Trem.: On, Fast

Music and Lyrics by
Randy Newman

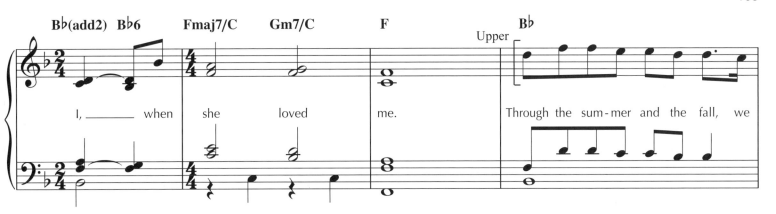

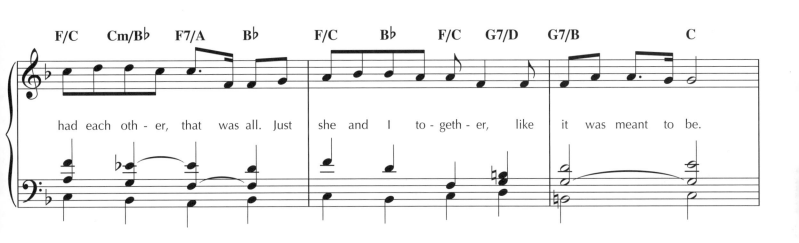

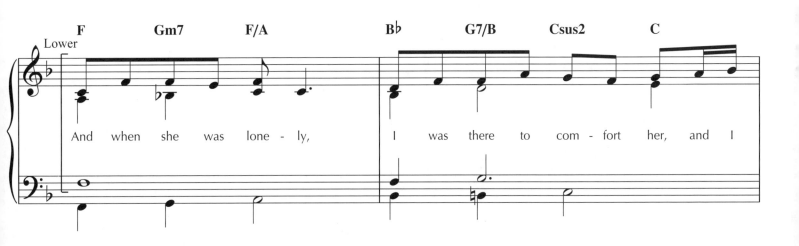

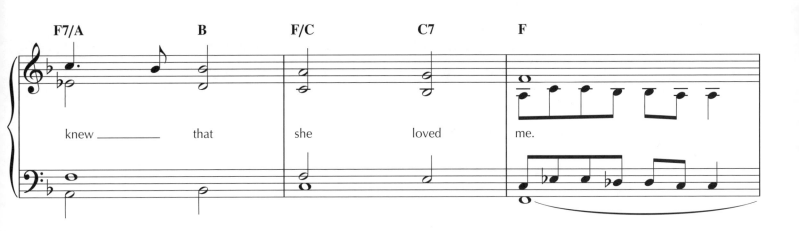

So the years went by; I stayed the same. But

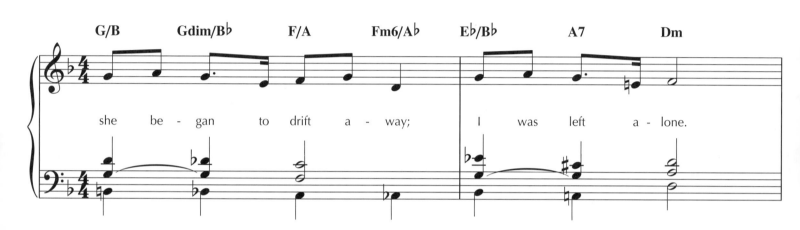

she be-gan to drift a-way; I was left a-lone.

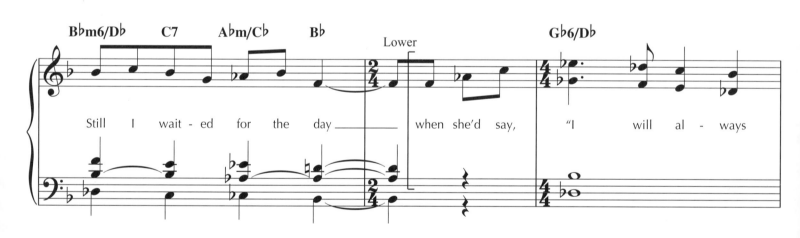

Still I wait-ed for the day when she'd say, "I will al-ways

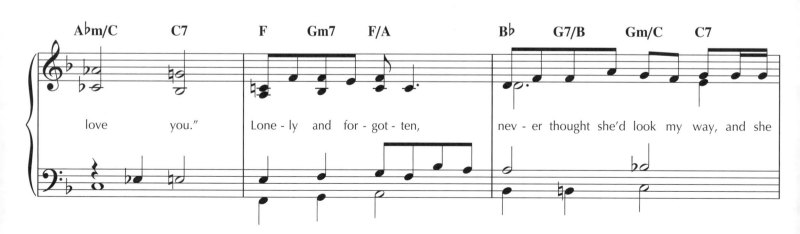

love you." Lone-ly and for-got-ten, nev-er thought she'd look my way, and she

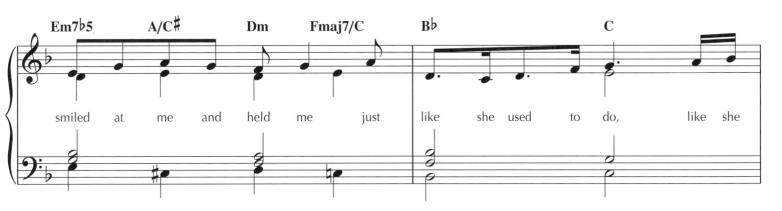

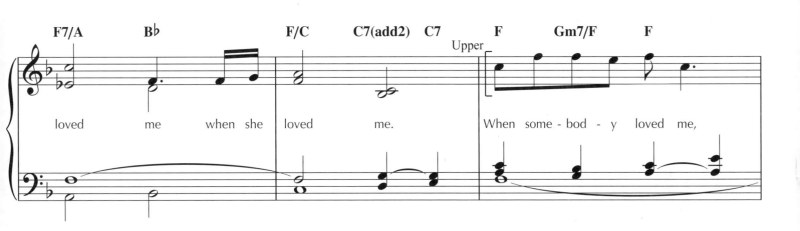

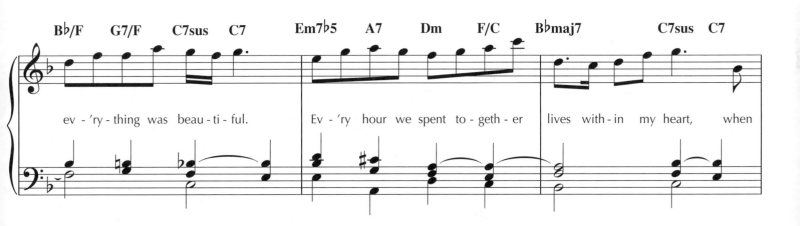

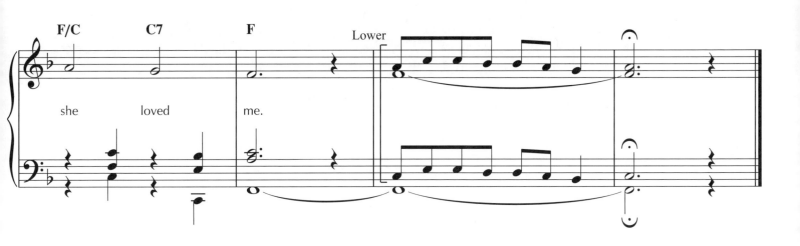

Wishing You Were Somehow Here Again

from THE PHANTOM OF THE OPERA

Electronic Organs
Upper: Bells
Lower: Strings 8', 4'
Pedal: 16', 8'
Vib./Trem.: On, Fast

Drawbar Organs
Upper: Bells
Lower: (00) 0702 011
Pedal: 24
Vib./Trem.: On, Fast

Music by Andrew Lloyd Webber
Lyrics by Charles Hart
Additional Lyrics by Richard Stilgoe

Yesterday

Electronic Organs
Upper: Flutes (or Tibias) 16′, 8′, 5⅓′, 4′, 2′
Lower: Flutes 8′, 4′, Diapason 8′, Reed 8′
Pedal: 16′, 8′
Vib./Trem.: On, Fast

Tonebar Organs
Upper: 86 6606 000
Lower: (00) 7732 211
Pedal: 55
Vib./Trem.: On, Fast

Words and Music by John Lennon and Paul McCartney

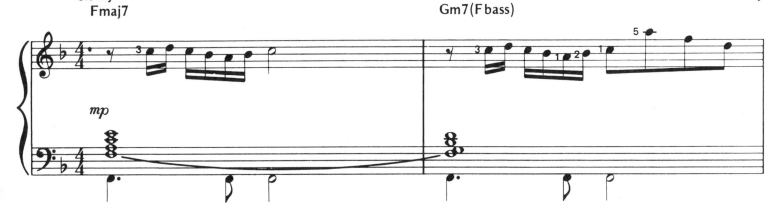

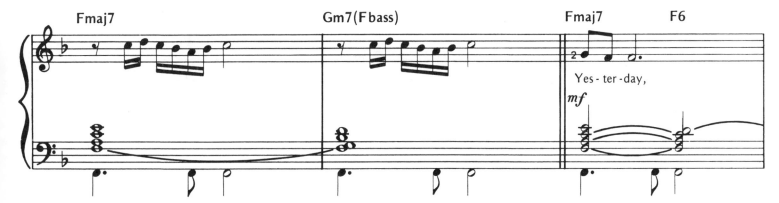

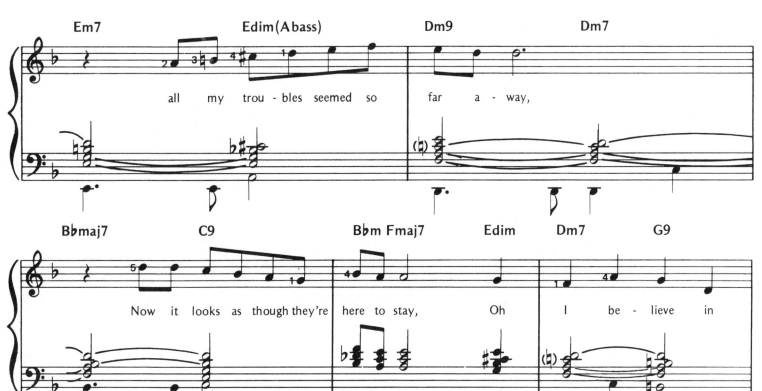

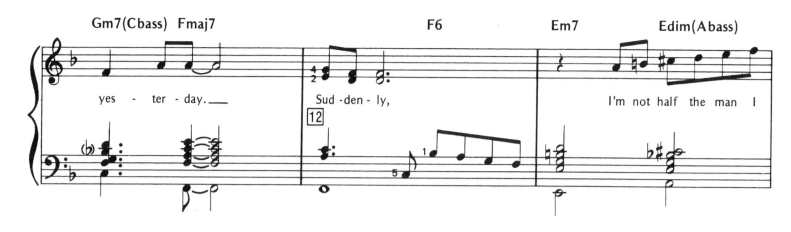

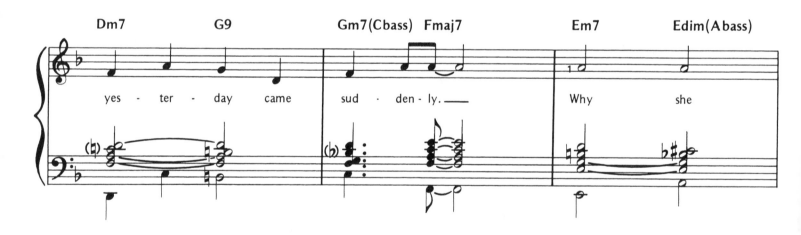

You Raise Me Up

Electronic Organs
Upper: Flutes (or Tibias) 16', 4'
Lower: Strings 8', 4'
Pedal: 16', 8'
Vib./Trem.: On, Fast

Drawbar Organs
Upper: 60 3616 003
Lower: (00) 56787 654
Pedal: 33
Vib./Trem.: On, Fast

Words and Music by Brendan Graham
and Rolf Lovland

seas.   I am   strong when I am on your   shoul - ders.   You raise me

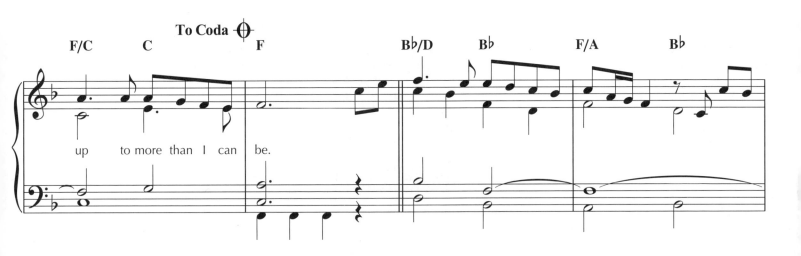

up   to more than I can   be.

You raise me

be.

You raise me   up   to   more than I____ can   be.____

GREAT ORGAN SELECTIONS

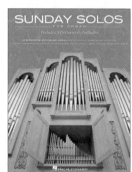

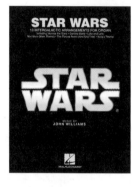

CHRISTMAS FAVORITES

80 Christmas classics every organist should know: Auld Lang Syne • Away in a Manger • Blue Christmas • Christmas Time Is Here • Dance of the Sugar Plum Fairy • The First Noël • Frosty the Snow Man • God Rest Ye Merry, Gentlemen • Have Yourself a Merry Little Christmas • I Saw Three Ships • It Came upon the Midnight Clear • Jingle Bells • Joy to the World • A Marshmallow World • O Holy Night • Rockin' Around the Christmas Tree • Silent Night • Up on the Housetop • What Child Is This? • White Christmas • and many more.
00144576 $14.99

CONTEMPORARY CHRISTIAN CLASSICS

12 songs of praise, including: El Shaddai • How Majestic Is Your Name • More Than Wonderful • Upon This Rock • We Shall Behold Him.
00199095 $8.99

GOSPEL TREASURES

35 gospel favorites for organ: Amazing Grace • Blessed Assurance • Higher Ground • I Love to Tell the Story • In the Garden • Just a Closer Walk with Thee • Nearer, My God, to Thee • The Old Rugged Cross • Rock of Ages • Shall We Gather at the River? • Sweet By and By • What a Friend We Have in Jesus • Wonderful Peace • and many more.
00144550 $7.99

THE MOST BEAUTIFUL SONGS EVER

70 beautiful melodies arranged for organ: Autumn Leaves • Edelweiss • How High the Moon • If I Were a Bell • Luck Be a Lady • Misty • Ol' Man River • Satin Doll • Smile • Stardust • Summertime • Till There Was You • Unchained Melody • The Way You Look Tonight • Witchcraft • and more.
00144638 $16.99

105 FAVORITE HYMNS

Hal Leonard Organ Adventure Series – No. 18
arr. Bill Irwin
105 songs, including: Amazing Grace • The Church in the Wildwood • Holy, Holy, Holy • and more.
00212500 $10.95

THE PHANTOM OF THE OPERA

Nine songs from the Tony-winning Broadway sensation that every organist should know: All I Ask of You • Angel of Music • Masquerade • The Music of the Night • The Phantom of the Opera • The Point of No Return • Prima Donna • Think of Me • Wishing You Were Somehow Here Again.
00290300 $14.99

SHOWTUNES

25 favorites from the stage to enjoy playing in your very own home! Includes: Bewitched • Blue Skies • Cabaret • Camelot • Edelweiss • Get Me to the Church on Time • Getting to Know You • I Could Write a Book • I Love Paris • Memory • Oklahoma • One • People • The Sound of Music • The Surrey with the Fringe on Top • Tomorrow • and more.
00199009 $9.95

THE SOUND OF MUSIC

A great souvenir collection featuring organ arrangements of six songs from the beloved Rodgers & Hammerstein masterpiece as well as photos, story synopsis and history of the musical. Includes: Climb Ev'ry Mountain • Do-Re-Mi • Edelweiss • My Favorite Things • Sixteen Going on Seventeen • The Sound of Music.
00217085 $9.99

STAR WARS FOR ORGAN

A baker's dozen of John Williams' masterful themes for *Star Wars* movies in grand arrangements for organ: Across the Stars (Love Theme from *Attack of the Clones*) • Cantina Band • Duel of the Fates • Farewell and the Trip • The Imperial March (Darth Vader's Theme) • Luke and Leia • March of the Resistance • May the Force Be with You • Princess Leia's Theme • Rey's Theme • Star Wars (Main Theme) • The Throne Room (And End Title) • Yoda's Theme.
00157400 $16.99

SUNDAY SOLOS FOR ORGAN

Preludes, Offertories & Postludes
Contains 30 blended selections perfect for organists to play every Sunday: Abide with Me • El Shaddai • He Is Exalted • Holy Ground • Lamb of Glory • A Mighty Fortress Is Our God • Rock of Ages • Via Dolorosa • What a Friend We Have in Jesus • and more.
00199016 $14.99

WONDERFUL STANDARDS

Take a trip down memory lane with these 25 gems arranged for organ: After You've Gone • Ain't Misbehavin' • Autumn Leaves • Bluesette • Body and Soul • Dinah • The Girl from Ipanema • How Deep Is the Ocean • How Insensitive • I Should Care • I've Got You Under My Skin • My Favorite Things • My Romance • Red Roses for a Blue Lady • September Song • So Nice (Summer Samba) • Watch What Happens • Younger Than Springtime • and more.
00199011 $9.95